DICATE EVANGELIVM OMNI C

BARTHOLOMÆVS   IOANNES IACO   SIMON CANANE

MATTHÆVS   THOMAS

Discovering the Bible
The Road
to
Damascus
and other New Testament stories

Retold by *Victoria Parker*

❖

Consultant *Janet Dyson*

DISCOVERING THE BIBLE

THE ROAD
to
DAMASCUS
and other New Testament stories

RETOLD BY *Victoria Parker* ❖ CONSULTANT *Janet Dyson*

LORENZ BOOKS

First published in 2000 by Lorenz Books
© Anness Publishing Limited 2000
Lorenz Books is an imprint of
Anness Publishing Limited
Hermes House
88-89 Blackfriars Road
London SE1 8HA

This edition distributed in Canada by
Raincoast Books
8680 Cambie Street
Vancouver
British Columbia V6P 6M9

A CIP catalogue record for this book is available from the
British Library.

Publisher: Joanna Lorenz
Managing Editor: Gilly Cameron Cooper
Senior Editor: Lisa Miles

Produced by Miles Kelly Publishing Limited
Publishing Director: Jim Miles
Editorial Director: Paula Borton
Art Director: Clare Sleven
Project Editor: Neil de Cort
Editorial Assistant: Simon Nevill
Designer: Jill Mumford
Copy Editing & Information Author: AD Publishing Services
Artwork Commissioning: Suzanne Grant and Lynne French
Picture Research: Kate Miles and Janice Bracken,
Lesley Cartlidge and Libbe Mella
Indexing: Janet De Saulles
Design Consultant and Cover Design: Sarah Ponder
Education Consultant: Janet Dyson

PHOTOGRAPHIC CREDITS
Page 6 (BL) John Hatt/ Hutchison Library; 10 (BR) Sonia Halliday
Photographs; 14 (BL) Michael Nicholson/ CORBIS; 20 (BL) Sonia
Halliday Photographs; 23 (BC) Sonia Halliday Photographs; 24 (BR)
Hanan Isachar/ CORBIS; 26 (BC) Jane Taylor/ Sonia Halliday
Photographs; 29 (BR) F.H.C. Birch/ Sonia Halliday Photographs; 30
(BR) Neil Beer/ CORBIS; 37 (BR) Arte & Immagini/ CORBIS; 41
(BC) Sonia Halliday Photographs; 51 (BC) Sonia Halliday
Photographs; 57 (BL) Historical Picture Archive/ CORBIS; 58 (BL)
Bettmann/ CORBIS, (CR) Arte & Immagini/ CORBIS; 59 (C) Archivo
Iconografico, S.A./ CORBIS, (CR) Julian Calder/ CORBIS; 60 (CL)
Archivo Iconografico, S.A./ CORBIS, (C) The Salvation Army
International Heritage Centre; 61 (BR) Paul Velasco/ CORBIS.
All other images from the Miles Kelly Archive

The Publishers would like to thank the following artists:
Studio Galante (Virgil Pomfret Agency)
L.R. Galante   Manuela Cappon
Alessandro Menchi   Francesco Spadoni
Also
Sally Holmes   Terry Riley   Sue Stitt
Rob Sheffield   Mike Saunders   John James
Vanessa Card   Andrew Robinson   (Temple Rogers)

Maps by Martin Sanders
Printed and bound in Singapore
1 3 5 7 9 10 8 6 4 2

Contents

Introduction

WHEN Jesus died at the time of the Jewish Passover, there were many people who hoped that they would hear no more of His teaching, which had challenged so many established ideas. The apostles, Jesus's closest followers, were disillusioned and disappointed. Their hopes had been dashed.

With the news of His resurrection, hope returned to the apostles, and fear to the authorities. Yet it was scarcely believable. The apostles struggled to make sense of the resurrection. The authorities explained it away or ridiculed it. Then something amazing happened.

It was another Jewish Festival, 50 days after Passover, the festival of Pentecost. The apostles had been told to wait for an event which they would only recognize when it happened. That day God came upon them in a way they had never known before. They felt His presence and were filled with boldness to preach the message of Jesus.

Foreign gods
This is the Temple of Apollo in modern Turkey. The apostles met great resistance from some people on their travels. All the places they visited already had gods of their own, with great temples built in honour of them, such as this one. They did not want to give up the gods they had been worshipping, sometimes for thousands of years.

The Christian church was born. It got off to a flying start, there were 3,000 conversions in a single day. The authorities soon cracked down, though. Prison awaited the disciples when excited crowds rioted after a spectacular healing. It did not deter them or the growing numbers who recognized the real hand of God upon the apostles.

Just as the church was getting itself organized, and people were learning to share responsibility and to meet for worship regularly, Stephen, one of the strongest of the new believers, was arrested, tried and stoned to death for blasphemy. Christians fled in all directions as, flushed with success, the authorities made one last effort to stamp out the Christian church for good. However, not even prison could stop the disciples preaching – especially when, on a couple of occasions, the apostles were freed in what could only be described as a miracle. One disciple, Philip, fled north to Samaria and led a

Paul's base of operations
Ephesus was, at this time, the most important city in the Roman province of Asia, in what is modern Turkey. Paul's final missionary journey had Ephesus as its goal, and he stayed there for over two years. He eventually made Ephesus the base for bringing Christianity to the whole region.

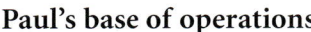

powerful mission in which many people turned to Christ. Others, not named, spoke about the gospel wherever they went, starting small communities of Christians across Judea, Syria and beyond.

Leading the opposition campaign was a Pharisee named Saul. Well learned in the scriptures, he knew all the stories about God's powerful deeds in the past. Little did he expect to experience one for himself. Thrown to the ground by a thunderbolt, blinded by a heavenly light, he was confronted by the risen Christ Himself and was suddenly converted to Christianity.

The new convert to Christianity used his Roman name, Paul, from then on as a sign of his change. After a period of study and reflection, thinking about his experiences, he was found by one of the church leaders, Barnabas, and called in to help the church at Antioch in Syria. It became his base, and from there he set off on three remarkable missionary journeys.

He trekked on foot and by sea all over what is now Asia Minor and Greece, starting churches and looking after the new converts. Although a Jew himself, he became the apostle to the Gentiles, the non-Jewish people, but he was not the first to recognise their rightful place in Jesus's church. That had been Peter, the leader of the apostles since the crucifixion of Jesus.

After an eventful life in which he was shipwrecked several times, beaten by persecutors and muggers, stoned almost to death, and suffering illnesses and deprivation, Paul was finally arrested and shipped to Rome for trial before the Emperor Nero. The remainder of his life is uncertain, except that he was executed some four years after his arrival in Rome.

While he travelled, he also wrote thirteen of the New Testament books. These were mostly letters to people he had met, but they included a couple of essays on religion. He was not the only one to write, however. The New Testament ends with a remarkable vision, written by John, full of powerful symbolism, about the state of the world in the period between Christ's resurrection and future return. The book captures the hope of the first Christians which caused them to face appalling hardships, persecution and the threat of death, all for the sake of Jesus Christ.

❧ THE EARLY CHURCH ❧

This is the history of the early Christian Church, the acts of the apostles in the time after Jesus's death

THE EARLY CHURCH
Acts Ch. 1 to 5, Ch 9 to 13.
PETER'S JOURNEYS
Acts Ch. 3 to 5.
THE FIRST CHRISTIAN MARTYR
Acts Ch. 6.
THE CONVERSION OF SAUL
Acts Ch. 8 & 9.
PAUL'S MISSIONARY JOURNEYS
Acts Ch. 11, 13 to 28.
THE VISION OF JOHN
Revelation.

The Book of Revelation
Tradition says that the last book in the New Testament was written by the apostle John, shown here, who also wrote the fourth Gospel. The book is described as apocalyptic. This means that it says that God will eventually intervene and destroy the world to bring about his will. The book uses lots of symbolism, such as describing evil as a horned beast.

The Early Church

THE EARLY CHRISTIAN CHURCH was mainly concerned with evangelism. This means that the disciples wanted to travel around the world and spread the teachings of Jesus to as many people as they could.

They started in the area around Jerusalem, where Jesus had spent His final days. As time went on, though, they travelled further and further afield, covering most of the eastern area of the Mediterranean Sea. Much of their work was in Asia Minor, an area now mostly covered by Turkey, but they also travelled to Greece, as well as many of the islands in the Mediterranean, such as Cyprus and Crete.

Rome

Puteoli

Pompeii

ADRIATIC SEA

Thessalonika

CORFU

Delphi

Athens

Corinth

Carthage

Syracuse

MALTA

MEDITERRANEAN SEA

Cyrene

BLACK SEA

Ancyra

Iconium

Ephesus

Miletus

Derbe

Tarsus

Antioch

Myra

Rhodes

CYPRUS

Salamis

Salmone

CRETE

Paphos

Sidon

Damascus

Lasea

MEDITERRANEAN SEA

Caesarea

Jerusalem

Alexandria

Memphis

Twelve Once More

AFTER Jesus had been taken up into heaven, the disciples followed His instructions and went back to Jerusalem to wait for the Holy Spirit to come and baptize them. The friends were more than a little nervous. They had seen many extraordinary things since they had met Jesus. His miraculous return from the dead had crowned everything. Even so, the disciples couldn't imagine how the Holy Spirit would visit them, and they had no idea when it might happen. Still, the amazing events since Jesus's death had inspired new faith in the disciples. They realized that everything Jesus had ever said would happen had come to pass just as He had foretold. Even though Jesus was no longer among the disciples, their belief in Him and His teachings was unshakeable. They didn't doubt for one second that Jesus would one day come back to the world in all His glory, to establish God's kingdom on earth.

While the disciples were waiting for the Holy Spirit, they gathered together in a house in Jerusalem with Jesus's mother, Mary, the other women who had been close friends of Jesus, Jesus's brothers and many dedicated followers – about 120 people in all. Everyone thought it best to lie low for a while. Now that the officials had succeeded in having Jesus executed, they were looking for an excuse to wipe out all His followers, too. They

Tree of life
This engraving from the 1500s shows Jesus being crucified on the Tree of Life. The tree was said to be growing in the Garden of Eden. John sees a vision of it in Heaven, as he describes in the book of Revelation. It is a symbol of God's eternal life, a way of saying that Jesus lives for ever.

The light of the world
The disciples' message was that Jesus was the only way to God. Jesus had called Himself the light of the world, that is, the one who shows people the way to God. In this painting by English painter Holman Hunt, Jesus 'the light of the world' is standing outside the door of someone's life, waiting to be invited in.

were determined to stop the spread of Jesus's teachings, which they felt sure were leading people away from the law of Moses. So Jesus's followers kept out of the way of any possible trouble, and devoted themselves to praying.

There was just one thing that Peter felt had to be done.

"Jesus chose twelve of us to be His special helpers – one for each of the twelve tribes of Israel," Peter reminded the disciples one day. "Now there are only eleven of us."

The disciples hung their heads in shame and sadness as they remembered how Judas Iscariot had betrayed Jesus. Judas had waited until Jesus was in a quiet, vulnerable spot, then he had led the authorities straight to Him so they could arrest Him, all for 30 pieces of silver.

"Yes," the disciples agreed. "You are right, Peter. We feel it is what Jesus wants us to do. Who should we pick?"

> ❝ *And they cast lots for them,*
> *and the lot fell on Matthias;*
> *and he was enrolled with*
> *the eleven disciples.* ❞

The friends prayed and discussed, discussed and prayed, and finally agreed that the new disciple should be someone like them. They wanted someone who had followed Jesus right from the time when His cousin John first baptized Him and He started to teach, to the moment when He was taken up to heaven.

Out of all Jesus's followers, there were only two men who would do – Joseph and Matthias. Deciding between them was a very serious business. The disciples had to be absolutely sure that they chose the man that Jesus wanted. They prayed long and hard for guidance, and in the end Matthias was chosen. The disciples were twelve again.

THE DISCIPLES PRAYED HARD FOR GUIDANCE. GOD LEADS HIS PEOPLE, BUT IT IS NOT ALWAYS EASY TO FIND OUT WHAT HE WANTS. PRAYER IS A WAY OF OPENING OURSELVES TO GOD AND HIS WILL.

Christian baptism
Baptism is a ceremony in which a person is sprinkled with, or immersed in, water. It is a sign that God forgives and cleanses people of their sins. Sometimes it includes (or is followed later by) laying-on of hands to receive the gifts of God's Spirit. This tomb from the AD 200s shows the priest laying hands on a child after baptism in Rome. The Holy Spirit is represented by the dove.

❖ ABOUT THE STORY ❖

There was nothing magic about the number twelve, but it was an important sign to the first Christians. It showed them that God was making a new start. The Jewish race had started from the twelve sons of Jacob. The Christian Church begins with twelve disciples. The choice of the twelfth person had to be made by God, to show that the church was a spiritual fellowship, and not simply a human organization.

Tongues of Fire

THE disciples waited and prayed for a sign that the Holy Spirit was with them. Eventually, 50 days after Passover and the death of Jesus, it was time for the feast of Pentecost. This was the harvest festival when Jews celebrated God's giving of the law to Moses. As usual, Jerusalem quickly filled with Jews from all over the world who were coming to worship at the temple.

On the day of Pentecost itself, the disciples met together to worship. Their thoughts were suddenly disturbed by a rushing noise. They had never heard anything like it before. It was like a wind tearing through the room. They felt energy and passion blaze

through them. The twelve friends turned to each other with joy, and saw that a tiny flame was hovering steadily over each man's head.

"The Holy Spirit is with us!" they cried.

To their utter astonishment, they heard each other speaking in foreign languages.

"Praise be to God!" they shouted. "We are blessed with special gifts from the Lord!"

The disciples ran out into the streets. They couldn't contain their excitement. Some disciples found themselves yelling praises to God in Greek. Others were shouting prayers in Arabic. Some heard themselves singing hymns in Latin and Persian, and other languages besides.

> " ...we hear them telling in our own tongues the mighty works of God. "

The hoards of Pentecost worshippers passing by were startled by the commotion and stopped to see what was going on. A crowd soon gathered around the disciples. Egyptians, Persians, Greeks, Romans, Libyans, Parthians and Phrygians were all amazed to hear the disciples speaking perfectly in their own languages.

"Who are these men? They can understand and speak our language!" the foreign worshippers gasped.

Others simply scoffed at the strange sight.

"They're just talking gibberish!" some people mocked. "They must have been at the wine!"

At this, Peter called for silence.

Church of the Holy Spirit
Pentecostal churches encourage members to use the 'gifts of the Holy Spirit'. Their worship is usually very lively.

THE HOLY SPIRIT IS GOD GIVING HIS POWER TO PEOPLE SO THAT THEY CAN SERVE HIM. THE DISCIPLES HAD TO WAIT TO RECEIVE HIM. WE CANNOT ORDER GOD TO DO WHAT WE WANT. ❧

The fire of the Spirit
The disciples saw the Spirit as tongues of flame above their heads. This medieval altar panel shows them waiting for the flames coming from the hands of God. Fire was a symbol of purity. The Spirit purified the disciples so they could work for God.

"We are not drunk!" he yelled, his face lit up with exhilaration. "We are devout Jews and have been worshipping, just as we should do at Pentecost. This is the fulfilment of the prophecy of the prophet Joel," he cried.

The crowds scratched their heads as they tried to remember the Scriptures.

"Joel said that the time would come when God would pour out His Spirit over people and they would prophesy, and that in those days, anyone who turned to the Lord would be saved from punishment for their sins."

Many people in the crowd gasped and remembered.

"Israelites!" Peter continued. "We are Jews like you, yet we follow the teachings of Jesus of Nazareth. You all know that He was put to death unjustly. This was all according to God's plan. For God raised Him from the dead. We have seen Jesus alive with our own eyes! What has happened to us today is the work of the Holy Spirit flowing from Him!"

A murmur of amazement went around the crowd. It wasn't just Peter's rousing words or sudden ability to speak new languages that stirred them, it was also the disciples' happiness and passion.

"What do we have to do?" voices began to cry out.

"Be truly sorry for your sins," Peter roared. "Beg God's forgiveness in the name of Jesus Christ. Then you will receive the gift of the Holy Spirit!"

"Yes, we want to be saved through Jesus Christ!" shouted the crowd. "We want to obey Jesus's teachings!"

That very day, 3,000 people were baptized into the new Christian Church as followers of Jesus.

Judaism at the time of Christ
The first Christians were Jews or Gentiles, non-Jews who had embraced the Jewish religion. Some who were in Jerusalem on the day of Pentecost took the message of Christ to their home countries. Areas with a Jewish population are shown here in orange.

❧ ABOUT THE STORY ❧

Pentecost had originally been a celebration of the barley harvest and also of the 'first fruits' – the first pickings of the fruit trees. So it was a significant day when the 'first fruits' of the Holy Spirit – the people who became Christians – were 'harvested'. It had also become a celebration of God giving the law to Moses. Christians saw the Holy Spirit as God giving a new way of life to His people.

Peter the Healer

IN the days after Pentecost, the excitement in Jerusalem grew. Crowds came to hear the twelve preach and see them perform miracles in the name of Jesus of Nazareth. Every day more people believed that Jesus really was the Christ, the Son of God sent to save everyone from their sins, and that through Him all sinners could be saved.

One day, Peter and John were on their way into the temple to pray, when a lame beggar sitting at the Beautiful Gate called out to them, "Kind sirs, do you have a few pennies you can spare?"

Peter and John stopped and stared at him.

"Look at us," Peter said kindly. "We have no silver or

gold – but what we do have, I will give you."

Peter stretched his hand towards the beggar.

"In the name of Jesus Christ of Nazareth," he said, "get up and walk."

Peter took the beggar by the hand.

Immediately the beggar touched Peter's fingertips, he felt new strength in the leg muscles and joints that had been useless for so long. His eyes lit up and without thinking, he sprang to his feet.

He took a few steps, then a few skips, then a few jumps.

"I'm healed!" he yelled. "I'm healed!"

The beggar began to leap about and dance in delight. He followed Peter and John into the temple, praising God at the top of his voice. Worshippers hurried to see what the commotion was all about, and were astonished to see the beggar who had sat at the Beautiful Gate all his life.

The Beautiful Gate

Scholars are not certain where exactly Peter and John met the beggar in this story, but most think it was where the Corinthian Gate now is, on the east side of the Temple of Jerusalem. It led into the part of the temple called the Court of the Women. It would have been a good place to beg as many people passed it.

MIRACLES IN THE BIBLE ARE NOT ENDS IN THEMSELVES. THEY WILL ALWAYS POINT TO SOME TRUTH ABOUT GOD. IN THIS CASE, PETER USED THE HEALING TO PREACH ABOUT GOD'S SALVATION.

A time for prayer

The Bible tells us that Peter and John were going to the temple at prayer time, 3 p.m. At this time there were set times for prayer in the temple. The morning and evening sacrifices were at 9 a.m. and 3 p.m. and there were prayer times to coincide with these. There were final prayers at sunset.

Before long a great crowd gathered around Peter, John and the beggar in the temple courtyard.

"Why are you so amazed?" Peter asked the stunned onlookers. "Why do you look at us as if we're filled with strange magic powers? For it is God who has done this through us. The God of Abraham and Isaac and Jacob – and the Father of Jesus Christ – whom you put to death."

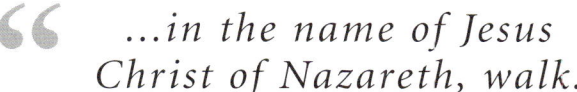

> **...in the name of Jesus Christ of Nazareth, walk.**

In a loud voice, Peter began to proclaim that God had brought Jesus of Nazareth back to life from the dead, that they had seen Him with their own eyes, and that it was their faith in Jesus Christ that had made the beggar well.

"Repent!" Peter cried at the crowds. "Turn again to God, that He may forgive your sins. Then, when Jesus Christ returns in all His glory at the end of the world, you will be blessed for ever instead of eternally damned."

The crowds suddenly fell back with fear. Temple guards armed with spears pushed through the people and marched up to the two disciples, followed by a group of angry priests and Sadducees, the religious elders.

"What are you doing?" the holy men thundered. "How dare you cause this rumpus in the temple!" They turned to the guards. "Arrest these men at once!"

Peter and John were hauled away to prison.

Statue of a sick man
This Egyptian statue dates from about 1200BC. From the Egyptians through biblical times there was little help for sick people. Many died young through disease.

Peter and John heal the beggar
This engraving shows the lame man just getting to his feet. Peter and John had only been able to heal him because God was working through them.

⚜ ABOUT THE STORY ⚜
Being a beggar was a miserable life. There was no social security system by which disabled or chronically sick people could get help from the government. They depended entirely on their families and the gifts of kind people. Peter and John could bring the gift of health and new life in every sense of the word – physical and spiritual. It was a sign that God was interested in every part of human life.

Arrested

PETER and John watched the sun set through a prison window. They weren't surprised or downhearted. Jesus had warned the disciples that they would suffer opposition and danger as they tried to spread His word.

After a damp and dirty night in the cells, the two disciples were dragged before an emergency meeting of the Jewish high council, the Sanhedrin.

"Now," Caiaphas the high priest said, holding them in his icy stare. "Tell us by what power or in whose name you healed this lame beggar yesterday."

It was more of a challenge than a question, just as if Caiaphas was daring them to say the name "Jesus Christ".

Peter remembered that Jesus had promised that He would give His followers the words to argue against His

enemies. Peter knew he was filled with the Holy Spirit, and he had a new courage to face the high priest.

Peter said, "We healed him through Jesus of Nazareth. You tried to destroy Jesus, but God raised Him back to life. He is the only path to heaven."

The elders leapt to their feet at the disciple's boldness.

"These men are peasants!" some of the elders yelled. "They are uneducated fishermen from Galilee."

> " *By what power or by what name did you do this?* "

"Jesus of Nazareth was intelligent!" others cried. "It's amazing he even spoke to these simple people. They probably can't even read or write."

"That may well be the case," others bellowed, "but the

Jerusalem is central
This medieval map shows Jerusalem at the 'centre of the world'. Jerusalem is central to the Bible story. It was where the first temple was built, where Jesus was crucified and where the disciples first received the Holy Spirit. From Jerusalem, the message spread throughout the world.

High priest's breastplate
The high priest, Caiaphas, would have worn a breastplate like this. It was studded with twelve semi-precious stones, one for each tribe of Israel. Inside the breastplate was a pocket, where high priests in Old Testament times kept the Urim and Thummim, sacred stones which may have been engraved with 'yes' and 'no'. They were used to discover God's will.

fact remains that somehow they healed the beggar. What are we going to do about this miracle?"

The councillors argued amongst themselves.

"Listen!" the Jewish officials spat at last. "We order you never to mention Jesus of Nazareth again or do any type of miracles in His name. Do you understand?"

"We understand," nodded Peter and John quite calmly, "but we can't do what you ask. We have to do what God wants us to do, not what you people want us to do."

At that, there was total uproar.

"How dare you defy the command of the Sanhedrin!" the enraged councillors yelled, and Peter and John were hauled away.

The elders were at their wits' end. They couldn't charge Peter and John with having broken any law and, to their immense frustration, they had no choice but to let them go with only a warning.

Back with their anxious friends, the two disciples praised God and prayed for strength and guidance.

"Lord, see how the elders have threatened us and grant us the courage to spread your gospel boldly, gracing us with the power to heal and perform miracles through Jesus Christ."

Despite the Sanhedrin's warning, the disciples carried on preaching and baptizing just as before.

Peter arrested
Peter was arrested on more than one occasion. This is an early statue showing him being dragged away.

Teaching the believers
Peter and John teach the early Christians. It is likely that as well as formal sermons, much of the teaching was based on questions people asked.

❖ ABOUT THE STORY ❖
The disciples knew they were doing what God wanted. The fact that they were performing miracles, and that people were finding a new spiritual life through the power of Jesus, were proof of that. The authorities found it hard to contradict them. The problem was that Jesus's body had never been found. The disciples could be right, Jesus really had risen from the dead and was there in spirit, helping the disciples in their work.

The Early Church Community

EVERY day, the Jews who had become followers of Jesus prayed in the temple and also broke bread in their homes as Jesus had done at the Last Supper, remembering Him just as He had asked them to do. Followers old and new told everyone how they had found new happiness and peace thanks to Jesus of Nazareth and how they had received the gifts of the Holy Spirit through baptism. Their excited neighbours and friends would beg to join the new Jewish group too.

Being baptized as a follower of Jesus Christ wasn't an easy path to follow. Jesus's followers were expected to follow the disciples' leadership and live as Jesus had done. This meant giving up everything they had previously held

dear. They had to sell all their possessions and give their money to the disciples to be donated to the poor. Most followers did this willingly. They believed that it wouldn't be long before Jesus would return in glory – perhaps a matter of months, maybe a matter of years, but certainly within their lifetimes. What was the use in holding on to their possessions? Besides, they felt they had changed inside when they were baptized. They embraced the idea that they were now part of a church, a community of brothers and sisters. They were happy to share anything they needed, and found comfort and fulfilment in being kind and generous to others instead of self-centred and thoughtless.

However, others found it more difficult to give up everything they had worked so long and hard for. A man called Ananias and his wife Sapphira obediently sold everything they owned after they were baptized. Yet when Ananias went to give the money raised from the sale to the

The church goes on
The word church simply means a gathering. Its focus is on a group of people, not the building in which they may meet. From early on, Christians have gathered together to worship God and to learn about Him. The pattern of services may vary greatly from church to church, and from place to place, but they all have the same end in view, the worship of God.

Church building
Early church buildings were not unlike many of those seen today, as this mosaic from around AD400 shows. During New Testament times, though, there were no special church buildings. People met in the homes of Christians, outside or in hired halls. Later the apostle Paul uses the image of a building. He says that Christians are built into a new community like stones are built into a temple.

disciples, he didn't take all of it. He and his wife decided to keep some back for a rainy day.

As Ananias laid down his sacks of money before the disciples, Peter frowned at him.

"Ananias, why has the devil filled your heart?" Peter challenged. "You are lying to the Holy Spirit and keeping back some of your money!"

Ananias and Sapphira had not breathed a word to anyone of what they had done. Ananias realized that Peter couldn't possibly have known, unless God Himself had told him! The terrified man stood open-mouthed and

> ❝ *And great fear came upon the whole church, and upon all who heard of these things.* ❞

spluttered. Words stuck in his throat, and he began to choke and gasp. A cold fear clutched at his heart and squeezed it with icy fingers. Then he fell down dead.

Sadly, the disciples carried him out to bury him. Three hours later, while they were still away, the unsuspecting Sapphira arrived.

"Where is my husband?" she asked, cheerily.

Then her face fell. Sapphira saw that Peter looked grim. She felt that the atmosphere in the room was stony. Sapphira realized that something was wrong.

"First, tell me how much you have sold the land for," Peter asked her.

Sapphira swallowed hard and lied about the amount, feeling her face begin to flush with shame.

Peter's eyes flashed fire. "Why have you and your husband joined together in sin?" he groaned. "Why do you think you can deceive the Holy Spirit?"

Sapphira hung her head.

"Listen," said Peter, growing angrier by the second. "Do you hear footsteps? They are the footsteps of those who have just buried your husband. They're coming to do exactly the same to you!"

With a scream, Sapphira fainted and fell stone dead on the floor.

When the disciples came in, they found they had another body to bury. All the followers who heard of God's wrath trembled in fear. How glad they were that they had found salvation through Jesus Christ! God's punishments on sinners were terrible.

Caring for the needy
The first Christians cared for each other. They were not afraid to sell possessions and give the money to help others. They did this because Jesus had given up everything, including His life, for them. They also believed God would bless them spiritually.

❧ **ABOUT THE STORY** ❧

This story shows how important honesty and truth are. Ananias and Sapphira wanted to appear generous. They pretended they had given everything but they hadn't. There was really nothing wrong with keeping some of the money for themselves. There was everything wrong with lying to Peter, and by doing so lying to God. Their harsh punishment reminded the Christians that they were to respect God.

Teaching in Jesus's Name

PETER became famous as a healer. People from towns and villages all over Judea began to put sick people out on the pavements, in case Peter passed by. They believed that if even his shadow fell on them, they would be healed.

The officials of the Sanhedrin were worried. Even though Jesus was dead, it was in His name that people were being stirred up. Even some of the priests had been baptized as followers.

"We must put a stop to this!" the officials raged.

Once again they had Peter and John arrested and flung into the city prison with murderers, robbers and thugs.

Peter and John weren't behind bars long. That night, an angel of the Lord came and released them.

"Go to the temple and tell everyone about salvation

through Jesus Christ," the angel told them, before he disappeared. That's exactly what Peter and John did.

Meanwhile, the Sanhedrin members were waiting for the guards to bring Peter and John before them. Caiaphas sat impatiently drumming his fingers.

Down in the dungeons, the guards were panicking. Peter and John were nowhere to be found. The baffled guards trembled with fear as they returned to Caiaphas.

"The prisoners have gone," the guards mumbled.

"What do you mean, gone?" the high priest roared.

The cowering soldiers shrugged.

"The sentries were on guard and the doors locked, but Peter and John weren't there."

Remains of Peter's house
These remains in Capernaum are believed by some scholars to be of the house where Peter lived. It was used as a church for some 300 years and later a church was built over part of it, which suggests that the first Christians thought it special.

Leader of the disciples
Peter was the spokesman for the twelve disciples during Jesus's lifetime and afterwards. He often spoke up when the others were afraid.

"Right!" screamed Caiaphas. "That's it! You're going into the dungeons yourselves until..."

Luckily for the guards, a servant burst in.

"Well?" snarled the high priest.

"My lord, we've heard that your two Galilean prisoners are preaching in the temple!" the servant panted.

> ## We must obey God rather than men.

Thunder-faced, Caiaphas sent his guards off to arrest Peter and John again, and the next day the disciples found themselves facing the fury of the Sanhedrin.

"We expressly forbade you to mention the name of Jesus of Nazareth!" the councillors screamed.

"We must do what God wants," Peter and John insisted. "God has filled us with the Holy Spirit so we can testify that Jesus is the Saviour of the world."

The members of the Sanhedrin were enraged.

"Put them to death!" the Jewish officials screamed. "They have no regard for us or our laws!"

One voice rose over the uproar. "Calm down! Take the prisoners away while we discuss things properly."

It was the Pharisee, Gamaliel, a teacher of the law for whom everyone had the utmost respect.

"Friends, listen," Gamaliel continued. "In past years, several so-called holy men have risen up and tried to set up religious sects to rival the worship of God. Look what happened to them. One by one they came to a sticky end and their followers were all killed. It is bound to be the same with this Jesus of Nazareth."

The Jewish officials murmured their agreement.

"There is another reason not to overreact," Gamaliel went on. "There is a possibility – although we are all agreed that it is highly remote – that Jesus really is who His disciples say He is: the Son of God. If this were true, nothing anyone could do would stop His followers. In the end, we might even be found guilty of opposing God!"

The scowling elders could see the sense in Gamaliel's words. Grudgingly, they agreed to let Peter and John go. However, first, they had the disciples beaten, and ordered them once more never to speak the name of Jesus of Nazareth again.

Reaching a verdict
The Sanhedrin was the Jews' supreme court of law. Verdicts were reached by voting. In Greek courts, jurors used voting disks like these, which come from around 300BC. Those with a solid hub meant the person was not guilty, those with a hole meant guilty.

Prisoner in agony
This silver and bronze figure shows a Libyan prisoner in Egypt between 1580 and 1200BC. Throughout history people have invented ways of hurting and torturing people they don't like, as the authorities did with Peter and John.

❧ ABOUT THE STORY ❧

Gamaliel's common sense saved the Sanhedrin from another miscarriage of justice. They had condemned Jesus illegally as they had not allowed a day to pass before a guilty verdict was announced. They were about to do the same again. Luke, who wrote this story, is showing that God was in control. Jesus had to die, to fulfil God's purpose. The disciples could not die yet. They had work to do for God to fulfil His purpose.

Stephen the Martyr

As the number of people who wanted to follow Christ increased, so did the number of helpers the disciples needed. The disciples chose seven men to distribute money and food and preach Jesus's gospel. One assistant, called Stephen, soon stood out as being especially learned and courageous. He was full of faith and the Holy Spirit, and had the power to work miracles. He spoke with such wisdom that the teachers in the synagogues found they had met their match. Eventually, the elders bribed people to say they had heard Stephen speak out against Moses and God. Stephen was put on trial before the Sanhedrin.

"We've heard this man Stephen say Jesus of Nazareth will destroy the temple and will change the laws that Moses gave us direct from the hand of God," people lied.

Stephen listened to all the lies without blinking or saying a word. His face grew bright and shone like the face of an angel.

The high priest tried to ignore the glow of Stephen's face. "Is this so?" he questioned. "Tell us now!"

The Holy Spirit helped Stephen speak. He spoke of the Jewish people, from the moment God had chosen Abraham to found the Jewish faith and guided him to Israel. Stephen said that God had sent Jesus of Nazareth as the fulfilment of His plan. In the past, the elders had persecuted prophets for speaking the truth, and they had done exactly the same thing to Christ.

"Jesus is the Saviour of the world, sent to you by God Himself," Stephen cried. "You murdered Him!"

The Sanhedrin were outraged. They exploded with hate.

To their immense annoyance, Stephen seemed totally unaware of it all. The young man stood gazing upwards, a blissful smile on his face.

"Look!" he gasped. "I can see the heavens opening!"

Stephen fell to his knees, oblivious to the riot around him.

"I can see the Son of Man sitting at the right hand of God!" Stephen gasped, with tears of joy in his eyes.

"What is this rubbish?" the Jewish officials yelled, looking up and seeing nothing but the bricks of the roof. Stephen's calmness enraged them even more.

"This man reckons he can see God!" the elders cried. "It's blasphemy – and the punishment is death!"

The officials clapped their hands over their ears so they wouldn't have to hear any more of Stephen's vision.

> *They chose Stephen, a man full of faith and of the Holy Spirit.*

"Take him away!" they yelled to the guards.

The soldiers dragged Stephen through the streets of Jerusalem and out of the city gates, with the furious Sanhedrin following, picking up rocks as they went. They reached the spot where stonings took place and stood Stephen up against a wall.

"Forgive them, Lord," Stephen murmured as the elders backed away. "Don't hold this sin against them."

The elders took off their cloaks and gave them to an eager young Pharisee called Saul to hold. Then they rolled up their sleeves and began to throw stones with glee.

"Lord Jesus, receive my spirit," Stephen cried aloud, as he sank down under the rain of rocks.

At last, Stephen lay dead. He was the first person to die in the name of Jesus Christ.

The stoning of Stephen
Stoning was the usual method of execution used by the Jews. Their law allowed it for many offences. Jewish law said the chief witnesses had to cast the first stone.

Stephen's gate
This street in Jerusalem is said to be where Stephen was stoned.

❖ ABOUT THE STORY ❖

Stephen was the first Christian martyr. The word comes from a Greek word which means witness. A martyr is someone who believes in his or her faith to the extent of being willing to die for it. During his trial, Stephen had spoken of the history of the Israelites in which people had regularly disobeyed God. Now, he said, they had ignored God's message once again, by crucifying Jesus.

Saul and the Christians

THE very same day that Stephen was stoned, the Sanhedrin decided that enough was enough. They marvelled that the followers of Jesus Christ were so loyal that they were even willing to die for Him. There were more followers than ever. Every day, the disciples were turning hundreds of Jews towards the new ideas of Jesus of Nazareth. The officials had to put a stop to the spread of Christ's word, and fast. They had tried ordering and threatening, and it had done no good. The Sanhedrin decided that force was the only avenue left.

Only a few hours after Stephen died, temple soldiers and the officers of the Jewish elders went marching into every house in Jerusalem, hunting high and low for followers of Jesus Christ. They upturned every house, questioned anyone who looked the slightest bit suspicious, and managed to haul off many followers. One of the keenest officers was the young Pharisee, Saul, who had held the Sanhedrin's cloaks at Stephen's stoning. Saul wished with all his heart that he hadn't been lumbered with holding the garments. He would have liked to have been able to throw a few stones himself.

Saul hated the followers of Jesus Christ with a vengeance. He had been brought up a very strict Jew and he felt that Jesus's disciples were busy undoing everything that he had always believed was important. Saul made up his mind that he would make the Sanhedrin's command his life's work. It didn't matter how long it took, he would

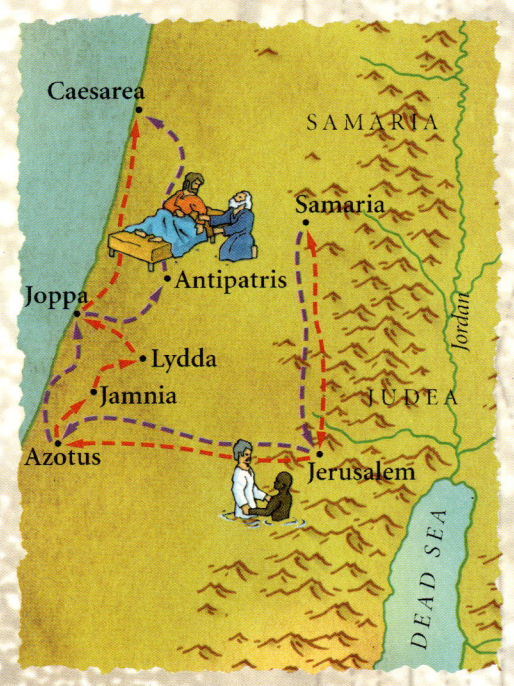

PERSECUTION IS WHEN A PERSON OR GROUP ARE MADE TO SUFFER FOR SOME REASON. CHRISTIANS HAVE ALWAYS FACED SUFFERING, FOLLOWING THE EXAMPLE OF JESUS, BUT THOSE WHO FLED SAUL'S MEN HELPED TO SPREAD JESUS'S WORD ABROAD. ❧

Early spread of Christianity
Jesus told the disciples that they were to take the Christian message to 'Judea, Samaria and the rest of the world'. The early chapters of Acts show how Philip (shown in mauve) and Peter (shown in red) travelled around the whole region.

Samaria
This city was despised by traditional Jews at the time of Christ. The city had existed since King Jeroboam had made it Israel's capital after the kingdom split under King Solomon. Herod the Great built a temple dedicated to the Roman Emperor Augustus there shortly before Christ was born.

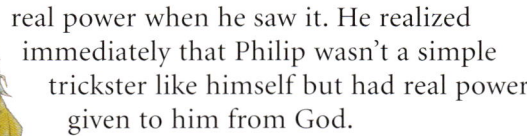

stop at nothing until every last follower of Jesus Christ was locked up, and preferably killed. Saul decided that he wouldn't stop at Jerusalem, either. After turning the holy city upside down, Saul commanded his disciple-hunters to sweep through the whole of Judea.

Never in his wildest dreams did Saul think that he was actually part of God's plan to spread the word of Jesus Christ. In forcing Jesus's followers to flee, the gospel was taken to many thousands of people who wouldn't otherwise have heard it. In every region the escaping followers passed through, they told the locals the good news of Jesus's promise of salvation. Jews everywhere begged to be baptized.

> *Now, those who were scattered went about preaching the word.*

The disciple Philip had great success in the city of Samaria. He preached passionately and worked great miracles. He healed those who were paralysed and cured others with terrible sicknesses that wracked their bodies with pain and tormented their minds. Crowds hurried to see Philip's amazing powers and hundreds were baptized. One of the new followers was a man called Simon, who for years had conned the locals into thinking he was a magician by performing tricks and conjuring. Simon knew

real power when he saw it. He realized immediately that Philip wasn't a simple trickster like himself but had real power given to him from God.

There were so many people in Samaria who flocked to hear Philip's message that he couldn't cope with the numbers, so Philip's friends and fellow disciples of Jesus, Peter and John, journeyed down to help him. When the two disciples arrived, they laid their hands on those who had been baptized and prayed that they might receive the gifts of the Holy Spirit.

"How amazing!" cried Simon, when he saw what Peter and John were doing. "You have magic in your hands! I'd give anything to have power like that!"

The ex-magician scrabbled through his bag and pulled out the last of his money.

"Look, take this!" he cried, holding out a handful of coins. "Give me some of your magic power, too!"

Peter turned on Simon in fury. He didn't often get angry, but when he did, it was terrifying.

"May your silver be damned along with you!" Peter roared, dashing the money to the ground. "You can't buy gifts from God!"

For the first time in his life, Simon was truly humbled before Peter. He made up his mind to make the most of what he was and not strive to be anything else or to envy others their special gifts.

"I am truly sorry," he said. "Please pray for me that my sins are forgiven through Jesus Christ."

Philip
God gave Philip the gift of preaching, to spread the Christian message and to bring people to personal faith. This mosaic from the 1100s shows him casting a demon from a man.

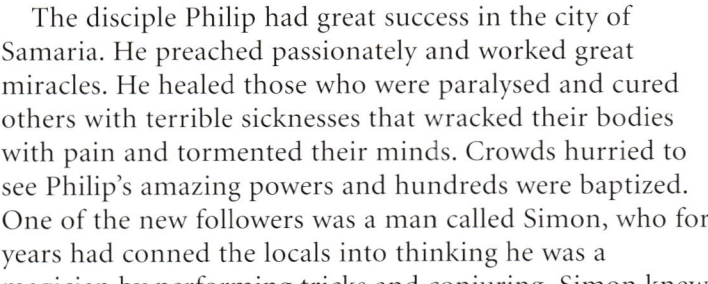

❖ ABOUT THE STORY ❖

According to Tertullian, a Christian writer in the AD300s, 'the blood of the martyrs is the seed of the church'. The church has grown most during times when Christians are being persecuted. This is partly because people decide that Christianity must be true if it is worth dying for. No one would die for a lie. It is also because early Christians amazed observers by their love for each other.

Philip and the Ethiopian

AFTER Peter and John had helped Philip in Samaria, they returned to Jerusalem. They preached the word of Jesus in many Samarian villages along the way. Philip didn't go with them. An angel of the Lord spoke to him and told him to go south instead, down the road from Jerusalem to Gaza. So, Philip obediently set off down the hot, dusty, desert road. He didn't know exactly where he was going, but he remembered that Jesus had said so many times before that God would always show the way.

As Philip trudged along, he saw a chariot come slowly rumbling by with an important-looking passenger inside. The chariot bore the symbol of the queen of Ethiopia, in Africa, and Philip realized that its passenger must be one of the queen's government ministers, who was returning home after worshipping in the temple in Jerusalem.

As Philip marvelled at the splendid sight, he heard a voice speaking to him, urging him gently.

"Philip, go and meet the man in the chariot," the voice said, and Philip knew it was the Holy Spirit.

Straight away, Philip ran to the chariot and greeted the minister with a respectful bow.

"Good afternoon," said Philip.

The minister turned his head haughtily. He was reading a scroll of the teachings of the prophet Isaiah, and he didn't look too pleased at being interrupted. Still he was well brought-up and polite, so he said "Good afternoon" back, before returning to his reading.

Philip didn't give up, though.

"I see you're reading Isaiah," he said, cheerily. "What do you think of it? Can you understand the prophecies?"

The minister was quite taken aback by the bold question. No one in the Ethiopian royal court would ever dare approach him and talk to him like that. He was just about to scold Philip when he noticed the kindness and honesty in his eyes. There was something about Philip that made the minister bare his heart and speak quite openly.

"No, I don't really understand much of it," the minister confessed in a whisper. "How can I, when I don't have anyone to help me?"

"Well, I understand it," said Philip, with a grin.

"Do you?" said the minister excitedly. "Do you really? Then you'd better come and join me."

Philip clambered up into the regal chariot and sat

beside the Ethiopian minster. Philip picked up reading from the point where he had interrupted him. As they continued the journey together he explained the Scriptures and told the Ethiopian minister all about the good news of Jesus.

> " *Beginning with this scripture, he told him the good news of Jesus.* "

The minister was entranced. Every word that Philip said rang true in his heart. The way of life Jesus preached was surely the only way to heaven. Jesus of Nazareth was surely the Christ foretold by the ancient scriptures!

Suddenly, the minister yelled "STOP!" at the top of his voice. The horses slowed to a halt and the minister jumped out of the chariot.

"Look!" he said excitedly, pointing across the road. "There's a pool. I want you to baptize me as a follower of Jesus Christ right away."

He grabbed Philip's hand and hurried him across the road as fast as his legs would carry him, splashing into the water. He listened intently to Philip's prayers, joining in with them in his heart. Then came the great moment. Philip dipped him down under the water and the minister was washed clean from all his sins. He emerged new-born, ready to begin a new life as a

follower of Christ. Philip was gone. The beaming minister looked all around, but couldn't find him anywhere. Still, nothing could dampen his spirits. He went on his way, singing God's praises and rejoicing at his new found faith and salvation.

As for Philip, he had been mysteriously whisked away by the Holy Spirit and taken to another town where he was needed to preach the gospel. He continued to preach the word of Jesus and convert people all the way down the road to Caesarea.

A Holy King
This minister was probably a royal treasurer for the queen mother. In Ethiopia at this time it was the queen mother who ruled the country from day to day as the king himself was thought to be too holy.

Ethiopian
In biblical times, the country of Ethiopia was in fact Nubia, which is now part of Sudan and Egypt, in northern Africa.

❧ ABOUT THE STORY ❧
The Ethiopian was a Gentile who had adopted the Jewish religion. He would not have been allowed to take part in Jewish ceremonies, because he was foreign. There was a Jewish community in Upper Egypt, from whom he had probably first heard about God. He is evidently very keen to find out more. This story shows how God met his spiritual need by inspiring Philip to be in the right place at the right time.

The Road to Damascus

THE YOUNG Pharisee soldier Saul had been having great success in his mission to wipe out the followers of Christ. Jerusalem's prisons were full to bursting with followers, all thanks to him. Saul was feared far and wide. Day and night, capturing followers was all he thought about.

When Saul had stormed from Jerusalem through every town and village in Judea, he went to the high priest and asked permission to extend his search to Damascus. The high priest gave Saul letters to take to all the synagogues, telling them that Saul had the authority to arrest whoever he pleased.

As the city of Damascus loomed in front of him, he rubbed his hands together eagerly. There should be plenty more followers of Jesus to hunt down there...

Suddenly Saul was struck by a flash of lightning that knocked him off his horse and left him cowering on the ground.

"Saul, Saul, why are you persecuting me?" a voice boomed.

"Who are you?" Saul stammered.

"I am Jesus, your sworn enemy," the voice roared.

Saul shook with fear. Deep in his heart, he knew it was the truth and he groaned aloud.

"Now rise," the voice ordered. "Continue into the city and wait there."

Saul sensed the light fading from all around him. He lowered his hands from his face and opened his eyes. Everything was pitch black.

"I'm blind!" he yelled, scrabbling around in a panic. "Help! Help! I'm blind!"

"Sir, whatever happened?" the soldiers asked, as they helped Saul up. "Why did you fall off your horse? What was that strange sound?"

"Did you not see anything?" Saul gasped. "Did you not hear the voice and what it said?"

"We heard something, Sir," the guards said. They looked at each other worriedly. Had Saul been working too hard?

Slowly and carefully, the soldiers led Saul into the city and found a room where he could stay. Saul would say nothing further to anyone. He wouldn't eat. He wouldn't drink. He hung his head, his sightless eyes gazing blankly

❧ ABOUT THE STORY ❧

This was a unique event. We do not know exactly what happened, except that Paul later said the people with him heard something, but did not see the light. Only Paul himself heard the full message and actually saw Jesus in the shining light. Paul later became an apostle – one who had seen the risen Jesus. Many visions of God include bright light, because light is a symbol of purity.

Thirteen disciples
This engraving shows thirteen disciples. Matthias has replaced Judas, and Paul (far left) has joined them. The disciples were the recognized authorities of the early church. Their teaching was regarded as coming from God.

at the ground, completely absorbed in his own thoughts.

Two whole days passed like this. The soldiers did not know what to do. On the third day, there was a knock at the door. It was a stranger called Ananias.

"The Lord told me to come and find you here," said Ananias, helping the wobbly Saul to his feet. "I know that you are the enemy of Jesus Christ, but He says that He has chosen you to spread His teachings – not just to the Jews, but to the Gentiles, too."

With that, Ananias laid his hands on Saul's trembling head. At once, scales seemed to fall away from Saul's eyes and he found he could see once more. Totally overcome with relief and joy, Saul fell on his knees and gave thanks to God. Then, to the utter astonishment of his soldiers, he begged to be baptized. He wanted to become one of the followers of Jesus Christ who he had sought to wipe out!

Saul, Saul, why do you persecute me?

Once Saul had got his strength back, he went to the synagogues in Damascus and proclaimed Jesus as the Son of God. People couldn't work out if the famous Saul,

persecutor of Christians, really had been converted, or if it was some kind of trick. At first, only the Jews who refused to believe in Jesus Christ decided that Saul was sincere. They felt that their greatest ally had betrayed them and, in their disappointment, they plotted to kill him. Suddenly Saul found himself being persecuted for the sake of Jesus Christ, just as he had persecuted so many others! Luckily, Saul heard of the plan and escaped.

It proved harder to convince the followers of Jesus that he really had changed. The disciple Barnabas, who believed Saul, took him to the twelve disciples. He told them what had happened on the road to Damascus, and Jesus's followers decided to accept Saul's amazing turnaround.

As an outward sign of his new inner life, Saul changed his name to Paul. He put even more energy and dedication into preaching the gospel of Jesus Christ than he had previously spent in the persecution of Jesus's followers. He was a highly educated Pharisee with extensive knowledge of the Scriptures, and won arguments against the most learned Jewish elders in Jerusalem. The former favourite of the Sanhedrin soon became the most hated. As soon as the disciples heard that the elders wanted to kill Paul, they sent him off to Tarsus, far to the north, to teach far away from the people who had become his bitter enemies.

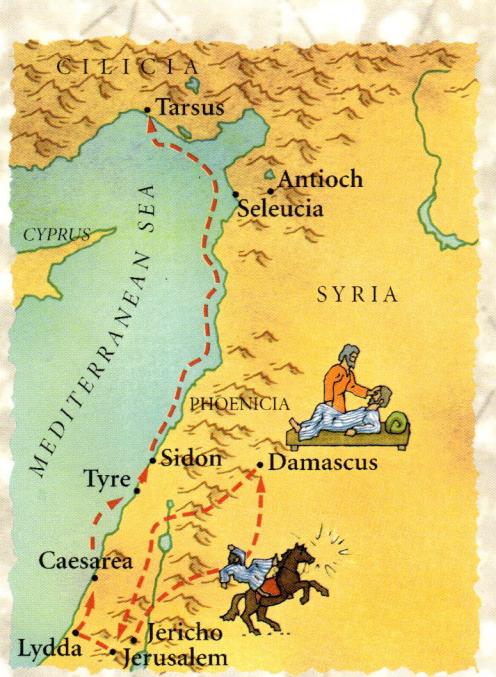

VERY FEW PEOPLE EXPERIENCE SUCH A SUDDEN CONVERSION AS THIS. OCCASIONALLY SOME DRAMATIC EVENT HELPS PEOPLE PUT THEIR FAITH IN JESUS. MOST PEOPLE GROW INTO FAITH SLOWLY.

Paul's journey to Damascus
Damascus is in Syria, the country to the north of Judea. In the first century, it was part of the same Roman province as Judea. It was about 240km north of Jerusalem and would have taken Saul several days to travel there and back.

Tarsus
This was Saul's home in south-east Asia Minor (modern Turkey). Tarsus was an important city in Roman times and may have housed up to half a million people. It was sited on important trade routes. These trade routes and its port made the city rich.

Aeneas and Tabitha

THE followers who had run away from Saul's persecution spread Jesus's teachings throughout Judea and Samaria, and into Jesus's home of Galilee. At the same time, the disciples were busy travelling from synagogue to synagogue, preaching the gospel of Jesus to large congregations of Jews and winning many believers by the miracles they worked in Jesus's name.

In a town called Lydda in the north-east of Judea, Peter was told about a man named Aeneas. All the locals respected him as a good and kind man. Aeneas had been very ill for over eight years and had become paralysed and confined to bed. His life had become a misery, with his healthy mind trapped inside a useless body.

"You must go and visit Aeneas," the people of Lydda

begged Peter. "The poor man has been terribly ill for so long. You are famous for the amazing healing miracles that you do in the name of Jesus Christ. We are sure you can cure Aeneas, too. Please help him!"

Peter went at once to Aeneas's house, and when he saw the faithful, God-fearing man lying in pain, he took pity on him straight away.

"Aeneas, Jesus Christ heals you," Peter said gently, taking his hand. "Get up now, and make your bed."

In front of all his neighbours, Aeneas swung his legs over the edge of the bed and stood up. Tears sparkled in his eyes. He flung his arms around Peter.

"I can walk!" he wept. "Praise be to God and all glory to His Son, Jesus Christ!"

A good example
Tabitha was a Christian who used her skills to help others. She was not known as a preacher, but she was known by her generosity.

Joppa
Tabitha lived in Joppa, which today is known as Jaffa and is part of the city of Tel Aviv. It is on the Mediterranean coast of Israel. It had been an important port since about 1600BC, although tradition suggests it was built earlier by Noah's son Japheth.

The celebrations at Lydda went on well into the night, but right in the middle of it all, two followers came hurrying from the nearby town of Joppa to find Peter.

"We've been sent to ask if you'll come to Joppa straight away," they begged Peter. "The people there are desperate for your help."

Aeneas, Jesus Christ heals you; rise and make your bed.

Immediately, Peter set off to the little town and arrived to find the sound of wailing filling the streets. A woman called Tabitha had just died and the whole of Joppa was in mourning. Everyone had loved Tabitha. She had always put others first, never thinking about herself. Tabitha was always on the lookout for kind, generous things she could do for other people. Almost everyone in Joppa had benefited from her kindness, especially the needy.

Tabitha had been a skilled seamstress, and she had spent her own money and time in making clothes for many of the poor. Now she was gone, her dead body laid out in the upstairs room of her house, and everyone was deeply sad. The people of Joppa had heard that Peter was near and believed that, working through Peter, the power of Jesus Christ could help.

Peter looked around at the weeping faces of Tabitha's friends and relations and called for silence. He knelt down beside the dead woman and prayed for a long time. Apart from Jesus Himself, only the great prophets Elijah and Elisha had ever been granted the grace to bring someone back from the dead.

Eventually, Peter opened his eyes.

"Tabitha, get up," he said firmly.

The people in the crowded room stood anxiously, scanning Tabitha's body for any signs of life. There was a gasp as her eyelids flickered a few times and then opened. Tabitha turned her head and looked straight at Peter. He stretched out his hand and beckoned, and Tabitha placed her hand in Peter's and allowed him to help her up.

The faith of the people of Joppa had been rewarded. Peter had brought Tabitha back to life, in the name of Jesus Christ.

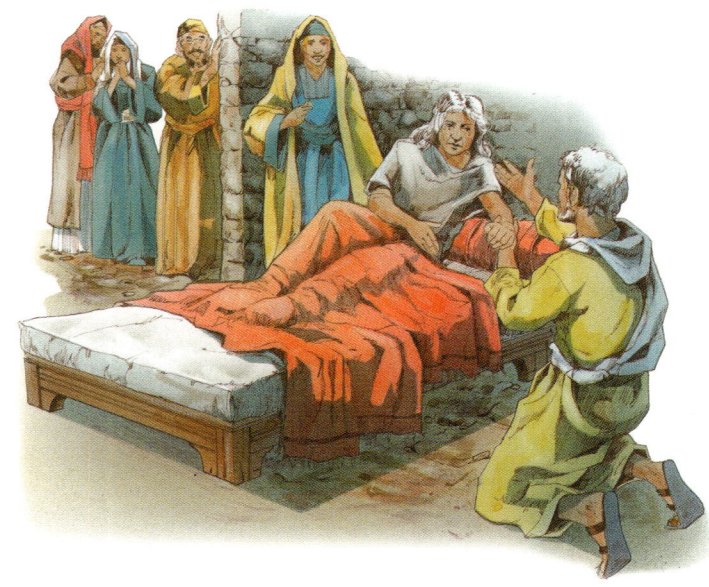

Spinning and weaving
In biblical times, many people made their own clothes. Wool was spun into threads on a spindle (which is what the woman on the left is doing) before being woven into a garment or a piece of cloth on a wooden-framed loom. Some people specialized in this trade and sold the cloth to others.

A devout woman
This statue shows a woman worshipping God. Tabitha always worshipped God faithfully.

✦ ABOUT THE STORY ✦

This story raises questions about God's attitude to suffering. Both Aeneas and Tabitha were well known as good people. Were they any more worthy of healing than other good people? The Bible suggests that people are not healed just because they are good or well known, but because God has a special purpose in healing them. In both these cases the publicity which followed the healing helped more people come to faith in Jesus.

Peter and Cornelius

It wasn't only Jews who were turning to follow Jesus Christ. Many non-Jews, or Gentiles, were showing a keen interest in Jesus's promise of salvation too. For a long time, the disciples knew that Jesus wanted them to spread the gospel to Jews through the whole world, but were not sure what to do about Gentiles. In the end, the Lord showed them.

After Peter had brought Tabitha back to life, he stayed in Joppa at the house of Simon, a tanner. One day, when Peter went up on the flat roof to pray, he saw the heavens open and a sheet being let down, spread like a picnic with all kinds of animals and birds.

"Kill something and eat it," said God into his mind.

Peter was horrified. He remembered all the Jewish laws about which animals and birds were considered clean to eat, the prayer rituals that should be said before killing them and the rules about how they should be cooked.

"No, Lord!" cried Peter in horror. "I could never eat anything unclean or not prepared properly."

"You must not consider unclean anything that God has cleansed," replied the voice, sternly.

The command was repeated twice, and Peter replied the same, before the sheet finally returned to heaven.

Peter was sure that God was trying to teach him something, but what? Peter's thoughts were interrupted by a voice speaking once again into his mind.

"Three men have arrived, looking for you," said God. "Go with them, for I have sent them."

❧ ABOUT THE STORY ❧

Peter had changed a lot since Jesus had risen from the dead, as had the other disciples. They understood God's purposes much better. They were still learning as they went along. This vision wasn't really about clean and unclean foods. It was about the disciples' attitude to people. In this vision Peter realized that the Christian message was for every group of people in the world, and that God no longer had a favourite race of people.

It is very easy to look down on people who are different to us. This story tells us that God regards all people equally, and so should we. ❧

"Gentiles – keep out!"
Gentiles were only allowed into the first of three courts surrounding the temple in Jerusalem. It was here that the traders sold animals for sacrifices, and where the money changers had their stalls. There were notices up all round the temple – this is one of them – telling the Gentiles not to go any further.

The bemused Peter obediently went downstairs.
"I'm Peter," he said. "How can I help you?"

"Our master, Cornelius, has sent us to find you," the three men began. "He's a Gentile, a Roman centurion. He's always been a God-fearing man. He prays regularly and insists that his whole household does the same. He gives lots of money to charity and all the Jews in the neighbourhood think very highly of him." The servants looked at each other nervously. "An angel appeared to Cornelius while he was praying and told him to send for you."

"Well, in that case, I'd better come with you," Peter said, and the three men smiled with relief.

The next day, the three servants took Peter and his companions to Cornelius's house. The centurion had gathered a welcome party of his family and friends. When Peter walked through the door, Cornelius fell on his knees before him. At that very moment, Peter understood what his vision of the picnic blanket had meant.

"Don't kneel before me," Peter said, helping Cornelius to his feet. "You're a man just like I am."

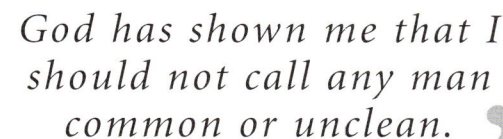

> *God has shown me that I should not call any man common or unclean.*

Cornelius was startled. He knew that it was unlawful for Jews to have Gentile friends and that special cleansing rituals were necessary if a Jew ever went into a Gentile house. Peter didn't seem bothered.

"I understand now that God has no favourites," Peter said. "He will welcome anyone who does what is right – no matter who they are or where they're from, whether they're Jew or Gentile, man or woman."

While Peter was speaking, everyone in Cornelius's house felt a strange glow in their hearts. They had been filled with the Holy Spirit, and they began praising God.

The Jews who had come with Peter were astonished. Yet Peter now understood.

"See?" he said. "Who can possibly say that Gentiles shouldn't be allowed to follow Christ?"

Cornelius and his household were the first Gentiles anywhere to be baptized.

❀ CLEAN AND UNCLEAN ANIMALS ❀

Jewish people live by a series of dietary laws, called *kashrut* or *kosher*. These laws set down not only which foods can be eaten, but also which foods Jews can eat with which.

LAND ANIMALS
The Jews were allowed to eat any animal that had a completely split hoof and also chewed the cud. This included cows and sheep. They were not allowed to eat camels, rabbits or pigs.

WATER CREATURES
All fish which had fins and scales were considered clean. They could not eat any sea mammals such as dolphins, or shellfish.

INSECTS
Only one kind of insect was clean: the hoppers (grasshoppers, locusts etc). All other insects could not be eaten.

BIRDS
Poultry and similar birds were allowed (the Israelites ate quails in the desert after they left Egypt). Most other birds were banned as unclean, including hunting birds such as eagles, gulls and owls.

Tanning animal skins
This shows Egyptians tanning the skins of animals, as Simon in the story did. Tanning made the skin into soft leather.

Peter in Prison

KING Herod Agrippa hated the growth of the church of Jesus Christ almost as much as Paul had done at first. The king knew that the followers drew great strength from their faith in God and the promises Jesus had made them. He feared them because of this. He was deeply worried by the way that the disciples had stood up to the Sanhedrin, saying that they obeyed only God, not men. Herod saw this as outright defiance of all human rulers and kings.

Herod determined to wipe out the followers of Jesus Christ once and for all. He ordered his guards to arrest Jesus's followers whenever possible. The king didn't stop at imprisonment. He had James, the brother of John, put to death. When he saw how this pleased the Jewish elders, and how he gained popularity among many traditional Jews because of it, he had Peter arrested and thrown into the dungeons too.

The only thing that stopped King Herod from executing Peter straight away was his concern not to be seen as a murderer. He had to be seen to give the disciple a trial first, even if it was on false charges and with bribed, corrupt witnesses. In the meantime, Herod kept Peter chained up to two soldiers – even while he slept – with a 24-hour guard outside his cell door. He knew how important Peter was to the disciples and he felt sure that the followers would try to come and rescue him. The king had also heard the strange stories of how Peter and John

had disappeared from prison when the Sanhedrin had arrested them. He didn't want that to happen again.

The night before Peter was due to stand trial and face execution, he dreamt that a strange light blazed into his dingy cell and that an angel was stirring him awake.

"Quickly, get up!" the angel commanded him.

Peter dreamt that the chains and shackles fell from his feet and he was no longer bound up to the snoring soldiers on either side.

"Dress yourself," came the angel's urgent voice. "Put on your sandals."

In his hurry, Peter tripped and nearly fell over himself. The pain felt real, but Peter was sure he was dreaming.

"Wrap your cloak around you and follow me," came the final instruction.

Peter followed after the gliding angel, right through the dungeon door and past the sentries who were all fast asleep at their posts, up the prison steps to the great iron gate. It swung open on its own, and the angel and Peter stepped out into the moonlit street. At once, the angel vanished and Peter felt a chilly breeze brush his skin. It hadn't been a dream after all! He was really free!

"The Lord has rescued me!" Peter realized.

He hurried through the deserted city to the house belonging to Mark's mother, Mary. Peter had to get to a safe hiding place before the sun came up and Herod's guards realized that he was missing.

At last Peter arrived in front of the little door. Knock, knock, knock, he rapped softly. No answer.

Well, it is the middle of the night, he supposed. Everyone is probably asleep.

Thump, thump, thump. Peter knocked a little louder.

Please wake up, Peter thought. Hurry up and let me in before one of Herod's watchmen strolls past and sees me.

No one came to answer.

> ## And the chains fell off his hands.

Bang, bang, bang! The desperate Peter hit the door even harder, and to his great relief he at last heard footsteps. The door swung open a little way and an anxious pair of eyes peered nervously out at him. The eyes widened in surprise and then a mouth gasped, and the door was slammed shut in Peter's face.

Peter stood shivering on the doorstep while he heard the sound of arguing voices inside. A few moments later, the door opened a crack once more and a whole host of faces peered expectantly out.

"I told you it was!" yelled a voice.

"It is!" someone else cried.

Then the door was flung wide open and Peter was ushered in. Everyone was talking at once and slapping him on the back, asking how he had got out of prison.

When everyone finally quietened down, Peter began to tell of his miraculous escape. By dawn, he was going over his story for the thousandth time. Peter's joyful friends wanted to hear every last detail over and over again.

Meanwhile, Herod's soldiers woke up to find Peter's cell empty. Shaking with fear, they went to tell the king – who was, of course, furious. Herod exploded with rage and ordered that every guard under his command to immediately go and search high and low for Peter. It was no good. Peter was well and truly gone. The evil king ordered that every soldier who was on guard that night would be put to death in his place.

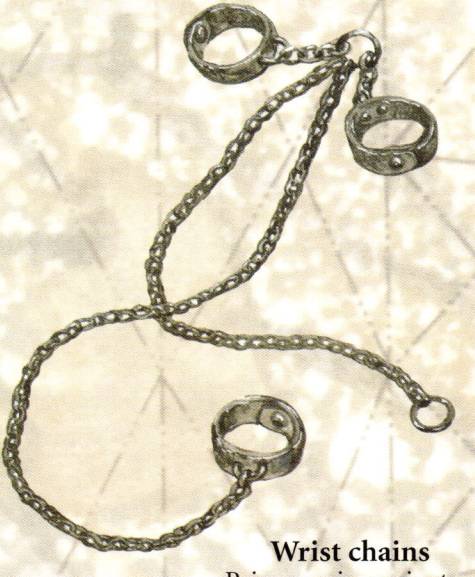

Wrist chains
Prisoners in ancient times were often chained to the wall, the floor or to each other. It was as much to shame them as restrain them.

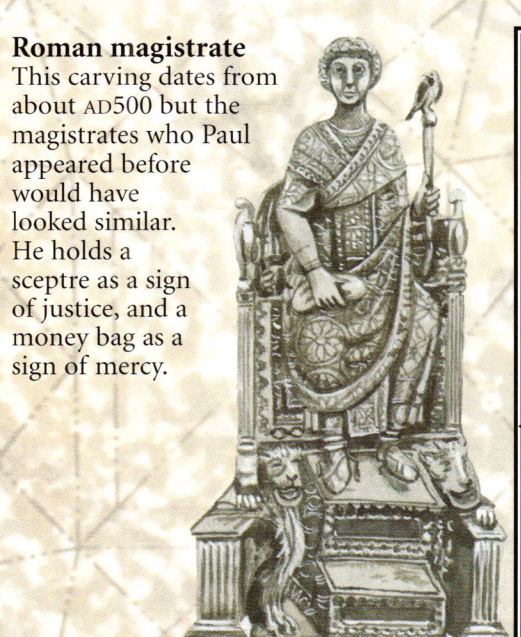

Roman magistrate
This carving dates from about AD500 but the magistrates who Paul appeared before would have looked similar. He holds a sceptre as a sign of justice, and a money bag as a sign of mercy.

> ### ❧ ABOUT THE STORY ❧
>
> *This story tells of a miracle. It was not the first or last time that disciples were released from prison in some amazing way. What matters is not how it happened, but why. This was a great sign to all the Christians that God did not intend to let His message of new life in Christ be chained up by non-religious authorities. He would find a way of letting it loose. This is saying that God is greater than any human ruler.*

Paul's First Missionary Journey

IN Jerusalem, the disciples heard that the followers who had fled Saul's persecution had spread the word of Jesus as far as Phoenicia, and the Greek states of Cyprus and Antioch. They decided to send Barnabas to guide them.

Barnabas went to Antioch first. He was met by so many eager followers that he went to Tarsus to fetch Paul to help him. For a whole year, Barnabas and Paul preached to the people of Antioch and baptized them. It was in Antioch that the disciples of Jesus were called Christians for the first time.

Paul was soon called by the Holy Spirit to sail to even more distant Gentile shores. Without questioning or hesitating, the disciple took Barnabas and John and several other followers to help him.

Paul's first port of call was the island of Cyprus. As usual, he and his companions began their preaching in the local synagogues. They worked their way across the island until they came to the town of Paphos, the home of the Roman governor, Sergius Paulus. He had heard about Jesus of Nazareth. The Roman governor summoned Paul and Barnabas to see him, so he could hear for himself.

When the disciples were ushered into the Roman governor's house, they noticed a pompous-looking local man sitting smugly next to him. Straight away the Holy Spirit told Paul who he was. His name was Elymas, an evil man who had set himself up to be a prophet. He had completely taken in the Roman governor by his magic tricks.

Paul and Barnabas tried to ignore Elymas and began preaching to Sergius Paulus, but the evil magician argued with everything they said, doing his very best to keep the Roman governor from believing in Jesus. Eventually, Paul lost his temper.

"You son of the devil!" Paul cried, in a fury. "Stop trying to waylay those who want to follow the Lord!"

Paul flung out his hand in Elymas's direction, and the magician cowered away in fear.

"Feel the true power of Jesus Christ!" Paul cried at the cringing man. "You will be blind for a time, unable to see the light of the sun!"

Immediately, Elymas's eyes grew dark, and he whimpered at the governor's feet in terror. Sergius Paulus looked in astonishment at Paul and Barnabas. From that moment on, he believed wholeheartedly in all they had told him about Jesus of Nazareth.

From Paphos, Paul and Barnabas and their helpers set sail once again. After calling at Pergia, they returned to Antioch, to see how the church they had set up was doing.

Paul and Barnabas were pleased with what they found. On the first sabbath that they preached, the synagogue was packed with Jews who had come to hear them speak of Jesus Christ and forgiveness for all. Even when they had

The first missionary journey of Paul
Paul did not make a circular journey. All the places he visited on the outward leg he visited again on the return journey, except for Cyprus. This took place about AD46–48. Paul never returned to Cyprus, but Barnabas went there with Mark.

finished preaching, the congregation followed them out into the sun, urging them to carry on.

All week, the Jews of Antioch spoke so excitedly about the good news preached by Paul and Barnabas that the Gentiles of the city heard of it too. On the following sabbath, the disciples found that almost the entire population of Antioch had turned out to hear them speak.

When the Jews saw the masses of interested Gentiles, they were extremely jealous of them.

> ❝ *In Antioch the followers were for the first time called Christians.* ❞

"You can't preach to them too!" they yelled, quickly working themselves up into an angry mob. "We're God's chosen people! No one can be saved unless they're Jewish!"

Paul and Barnabas stood firm.

"Don't forget that we brought God's message to you first," they reminded the Jews. "The Lord Himself has commanded us to 'be a light for the Gentiles, to bring salvation to the uttermost ends of the earth.'"

When the anxious Gentiles heard this, they were filled with gladness. They beamed with delight and gave thanks to God, and many of them were baptized straight away.

Yet the Jews weren't at all satisfied. They argued and scowled and grumbled. As the days went on, they grew angrier and angrier with every Gentile whom Paul and Barnabas welcomed as a Christian. All the wealthy men and women who had been very strictly brought up in the Jewish faith were particularly outraged. Eventually they demanded that the Jewish elders should drive the two followers out of the city.

Paul and Barnabas weren't downhearted. They had sown the seeds of faith among the Gentiles of Antioch, and they sailed on their way with great joy in their hearts.

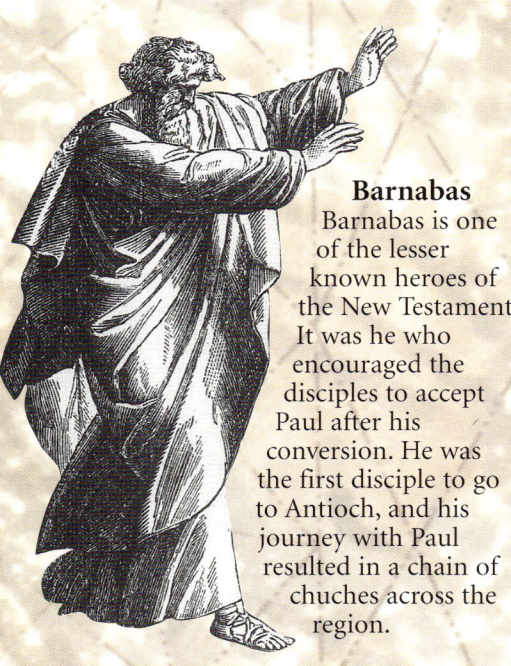

Barnabas
Barnabas is one of the lesser known heroes of the New Testament. It was he who encouraged the disciples to accept Paul after his conversion. He was the first disciple to go to Antioch, and his journey with Paul resulted in a chain of chuches across the region.

Cyprus
Barnabas came originally from Cyprus, as did several of the other disciples, so he was on familiar ground when he went back there with Paul. This Belgian tapestry, which is now in Mantua in Italy, shows Paul and Barnabas striking Elymas blind.

Faith for the Gentiles

PAUL and Barnabas being chased from Antioch was only the start of their troubles. In Iconium, Paul and Barnabas found that things were just as bad. They managed to win over lots people to Christ, but the traditional Jews felt outraged that Gentiles were being baptized. Paul and Barnabas were determined not to give up, but the situation grew increasingly difficult for them. People shouted them down in the synagogue and jeered at them. Eventually, the city was split into two sides who hated each other – those who supported the Jews and those who followed the disciples. When an attempt was made to stone Paul and Barnabas, they decided it was time to move on.

While many Jews were finding it difficult to accept Jesus as the fulfilment of ancient prophecies, many Gentiles

were finding it hard to give up the beliefs they had held all their lives. People had shrines to other gods in their houses and massive stone temples to Greek gods such as Zeus dominated the towns. It was hard for them to grasp the idea of believing in just one God and His Son, Jesus Christ.

When Paul was preaching in Lystra, he saw a man who had been a cripple from birth. Paul knew that he had the faith in God to be made well, and he suddenly broke off from his preaching and shouted: "On your feet!"

The man obeyed at once. "I can walk!" he cried aloud.

The gasping crowd stared at Paul and Barnabas.

"The gods have come down to us in the form of men!" they yelled, falling on their knees before the disciples.

"All hail to Zeus, the great father of the gods!" they cried at Barnabas, bowing down.

"All hail to Hermes, his swift, silver-tongued messenger!" they worshipped Paul.

❧ ABOUT THE STORY ❧

Paul and his friends did not think about going home when they were evicted from one city. They just went on to the next. Paul picked his cities carefully. He aimed for places where there was a Jewish community. If these people became Christians, then they could share the faith with their Gentile neighbours. He also aimed for cities which had roads to travel elsewhere. The message could spread out across a wide area after he had moved on.

Paul is stoned
Stoning was the traditional way in which the Jews executed someone for blasphemy, speaking against God. This ivory from the 900s is a representation of Paul's stoning. He was very lucky to escape – the stones could fracture a victim's skull.

The birth of Athena
Athena was the patron goddess of the Greek city of Athens. She was one of many gods worshipped across the Roman Empire. She was said to have been born from the head of the great god Zeus.

The two disciples were horrified. The men and women of Iconium hadn't taken in what they had been telling them about Jesus Christ and had interpreted the miracle as the work of their own pagan gods! A priest from the temple of Zeus came with oxen to sacrifice to them.

> " *...through many tribulations we must enter the kingdom of God.* "

"No! No! No!" Paul and Barnabas cried. "Why are you doing this?" The disciples stopped the priests and their followers just before they had time to slaughter the oxen. "We are not gods! We are humans, just like you! We are just the bringers of the good news that there is only one, true God, who made everything."

There were other problems. The angry, non-believing Jews from Antioch and Iconium turned up.

"Don't listen to these strangers!" they told the people of Lystra. "They're filling your heads with an evil load of rubbish! Don't listen to them!"

The Jews stirred up the citizens into such a frenzy of hate that a mob even went after Paul and stoned him, leaving him for dead outside the city. Yet as soon as Paul recovered, he and Barnabas continued with their work undeterred. They travelled far and wide, strengthening the faith of those who did believe. They also explained that Jesus had warned that those who wanted to enter the kingdom of God would have to face a great many difficulties and dangers.

Still, it was with relief that Paul and Barnabas eventually returned to their faithful following in Antioch, and rested there for a while.

Paul the letter-writer
Paul wrote many letters. The New Testament contains thirteen of them but he wrote more. The two letters to the Corinthians, the people of Corinth in Greece, refer to others which do not exist now. Some, like that to the Ephesians, were circulars, sent to several churches. Some were personal letters, like those to Timothy and Titus.

Inscription to the gods
People around Europe worshipped many gods at this time. This inscription was made by a coppersmith in Colchester, England. He put it in a temple to remind the god of his 'faith'.

Roman household shrine
People in the Roman Empire often had a shrine like this in their home where they would offer incense to their family god. The disciples had to explain that there was only one true God.

The Disciples Hold a Council

WHILE Paul and Barnabas were staying in Antioch, some followers arrived from Judea and began teaching the Gentiles that they had to adopt Jewish customs as well as be baptized if they wanted to be Christians. The two disciples argued with the followers, but the stubborn men refused to back down. In the end, Paul and Barnabas went to Jerusalem to tell the other disciples about the trouble, and to find some way to stop it.

Paul and Barnabas called the top Christians in Jerusalem together to a council in order to discuss recruiting Gentiles. When Paul told the council of the uproar they had caused by recruiting Gentiles as well as Jews into the church, the other disciples looked worried.

At once, some Pharisees who had been baptized as Christians agreed with the traditional Jewish view.

"It's true," they said. "It is the law of Moses. Only Jews can be saved. We are God's chosen people."

That was the start of a very long, heated debate. After all, it was an important issue that was in danger of dividing the church. Everyone felt strongly about his or her particular opinion. Finally, Peter stood up and called for quiet. Many people thought of him as the leader of the apostles, and he commanded a great deal of respect.

"Remember, friends," Peter began, "that God Himself told me to take the word of Jesus Christ to the Gentiles, so that they can believe in Him. I have seen with my own eyes that the Holy Spirit blesses Gentiles who are baptized, just as He does Jews. Why do you insist that only Jews can be saved?"

❧ ABOUT THE STORY ❧

The problem facing the church was whether Christianity was just a development of Judaism, or something completely new. The disciples decided that it was both. Jesus had fulfilled the Jewish law through His death. So the church was something new, not a sect of Judaism. The old ceremonies could not make a person right with God. People needed only to believe in God and in Jesus.

Jewish faith today
Some practices have changed little among Jews since Bible times. One of them is ceremonial cleansing. Jews wash their hands in a special way before they eat or pray. The person who lights a candle for worship may hold out his or her hands for cleansing.

Don't get drunk
A drunken man is supported by his friends. Paul advised the people of Ephesus that they did not have to abstain from alcohol, but they did have to use it carefully.

No one dared argue with the great disciple. Everyone kept quiet as Barnabas and Paul told about all the amazing miracles God had done through them among the Gentiles. Then James stood up and reminded everyone about the words of the ancient prophets: "'I will return, and I will rebuild the dwelling of David, which has fallen .... that the rest of people may seek the Lord, and all the Gentiles who are called by my name.'

> *Unless you are circumcised according to the custom of Moses, you cannot be saved.*

"So may I suggest," continued James, "that we stop troubling Gentiles who want to join us. It is God's will that they do not have to convert to the Jewish faith before being baptized in Christ. However, I'd like to propose that we give them some guidelines, so their fellow Jewish followers will not be offended. For instance, we should instruct the Gentiles not to have anything to do with pagan religions, to be faithful to their husband or wife and to prepare certain foods carefully."

Fortunately, this solution seemed to satisfy everyone present at the council. The disciples at once composed and copied a letter of instructions for all the Gentiles everywhere who wanted to follow the teachings of Christ. When Paul and Barnabas returned with it to the church in Antioch, the Gentiles rejoiced. They were finally officially accepted into the faith.

Marriage contract
James was anxious that the Jewish attitude to marriage should be followed by the Gentiles. This is because God had shown it to be His will for all people.

THIS STORY SHOWS HOW CHRISTIANS WHO DISAGREE CAN SORT OUT THEIR DIFFERENCES. THE DISCIPLES MET, HEARD THE EVIDENCE AND ARGUMENTS, AND PRAYED. THEN EVERYONE STOOD BY WHAT THE LEADERS SAID. THAT IS A GOOD MODEL TO FOLLOW TODAY.

Church council
This painting from Bulgaria shows the Second Ecumenical Council of the Christian church in AD381. Over the years since the meeting of the disciples there have been many important councils. As the world and people change, the church sometimes has to change to keep up.

Paul's Second Missionary Journey

PAUL and Barnabas remained in Antioch for some time, strengthening the faith of the church they had established there. Then the two men decided they should split up and revisit every place in which they had they proclaimed the word of the Lord so far, to see how the new Christian communities were getting on. Barnabas picked Mark to be his assistant and sailed away to Cyprus, while Paul chose Silas as his helper, and set off through Syria and Cilicia. In every town and city the missionaries passed through, they showed the churches the letter from the Christian council in Jerusalem regarding the baptism of Gentiles. Every day, the number of believers in Jesus Christ grew and grew.

Throughout his travels, Paul never planned his route himself. He always trusted God to show him where he should go. The Holy Spirit gave Paul signs in many different ways. One night, in Troas, he had a vision as he slept. He dreamt that a stranger stole into his room and crept silently up to his bedside. The man stood over Paul and stretched out his hands in earnest.

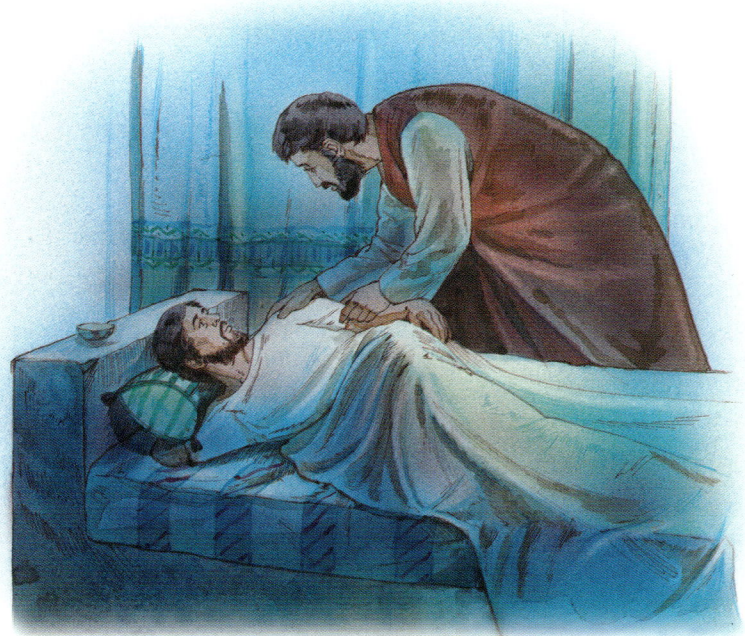

> " *The Lord opened her heart to give heed to what was said by Paul.* "

"Come to Macedonia and help us," he asked. Then the man's sad face faded away.

Next morning, Paul knew exactly where God wanted him to go. He and Silas gathered his companions and set off straight away to the Roman colony in the north of Greece.

Paul directed his little company of followers to Philippi, Macedonia's leading city. They found themselves in the midst of hustling, bustling streets, noisy market places, and buzzing shops and houses – but they knew no one. However, God made sure that He soon provided them with friends. The first sabbath that Paul and Silas were in Philippi, they went out of the city to a Jewish place of prayer beside a river. Many women were gathered there, and as Paul preached the good news of Jesus Christ, they listened eagerly. One woman in particular felt the joy of

❧ ABOUT THE STORY ❧

From now on, the story in the book of Acts includes many first-person accounts. It is believed that Luke, the author, was travelling with Paul for much of the time. This story also marks the parting of ways for Paul and Barnabas, and we hear no more of Barnabas again. The mission work increased, a sign that God was blessing it. Meanwhile, Paul's ministry was as powerful as ever.

Slave auction
This shows the harsh reality of the Roman slave system. The slaves had no rights of their own and could be bought and sold like cattle in a market. Many of these slaves were foreigners who had been brought to Rome as prisoners of war. A runaway slave could be executed if he or she was caught.

people to have their fortunes told. The two disciples weren't pleased at all. The slave girl followed them for days, crying out wildly after them wherever they went. Finally, Paul lost his patience. Without any warning, he turned and faced the slave girl, his face like thunder. Paul flung his hand out towards her and cried, "Spirit! I charge you in the name of Jesus Christ to come out of her!"

At once, the slave girl was quietened. She found she could no longer sense the strange unexplained things she had seen before. Her ability to see into the unknown had left her.

the Holy Spirit flood into her heart – a seller of fine cloths, called Lydia. Lydia begged that she and all her household should be baptized straight away, and she insisted that Paul and his companions come to stay with her during their stay in Philippi.

After that, Paul and Silas often returned to the river to pray and preach. One day, as they made their way there, they suddenly heard shouting behind them.

"These men are true servants of God!" came the shrill, excited voice. "They have come to tell everyone the way to salvation!"

Paul and Silas spun round to see a young slave girl hot on their heels, yelling as loud as she could and beckoning the startled passers-by to come and follow them.

The slave girl had a strange gift of prophecy, and her Roman owners were delighted with it. For years, they had made lots of money out of the slave girl by charging

Paul's second missionary journey
Much of Paul's journey was overland from Antioch and through Asia Minor. Paul told the Corinthians that he faced many dangers including bandits and fast-flowing rivers. He probably walked rather than rode animals.

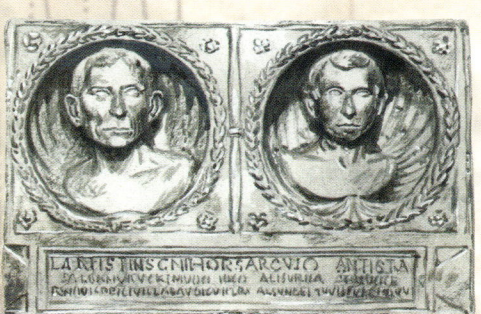

Kindly slave owners
Many of the first Christians were slaves. Not all slaves were kept in chains and badly treated. Some slaves were like trusted colleagues. Slave owners could, if they chose to, free their slaves (they then became known as freedmen) and some even continued to support them as patrons. This tomb was set up by two former slaves in honour of their Roman masters.

Paul and Silas in Prison

WHEN the slave girl's Roman owners found out that her fortune-telling skills were gone, they were furious. They dragged Paul and Silas to the local courtroom to make an official complaint against them.

"These foreigners are making trouble in our city!" they yelled, stirring up an angry mob.

The Roman magistrates didn't give Paul and Silas a chance to explain.

"Arrest them for disturbing the peace!" they ordered, waving forward guards to take Paul and Silas away. "Strip them, beat them and throw them into prison!"

Several hours later, Paul and Silas were locked by the feet into wooden stocks. Their skin bled from the Roman soldiers' whips and their faces were black with bruises where the guards had punched them.

Paul and Silas didn't let their plight make them downhearted. Instead, they trusted in the Lord and sang hymns to God. The other prisoners were stunned. Their God must truly be wonderful to inspire such faith, they marvelled. Some of them even joined in.

At midnight, the singing was suddenly drowned out by a mighty rumbling under the earth. The prison floor shook and the walls crumbled. The floor heaved, throwing the prisoners from side to side, breaking their chains and bursting open the prison doors.

When the earthquake had stopped, the terrified jailer ran in, expecting to find his prisoners escaped. All the torches had gone out, and he could see no one. The jailer drew his sword, ready to kill himself rather than face punishment for having allowed all the prisoners to escape.

Paul and Silas were horrified when they realized what the ashamed jailer was about to do.

> *Let them come themselves*
> *and take us out.*

"No! Don't! We are all here!" Paul cried.

The jailer couldn't believe his ears.

"Torches!" he cried, as guards ran in.

The jailer was amazed at the two followers of Jesus Christ. They had worked a strange miracle on a slave girl. They had been unaffected by being whipped and thrown into prison. They were unafraid of an earthquake. They made sure all the prisoners stayed in jail when they had had a chance to escape! The jailer made up his mind.

Rumbling under the earth
An earthquake happens when the pressure on two sections of the earth's crust causes the earth to split open.

Lock and key
Most doors were locked with bolts which slid across them, but the Romans also used locks and keys not unlike those we use today. This bronze lock would have been used for a small box.

Certificate of citizenship
The only way to prove you were a Roman citizen was to have an official document. This document is etched into bronze. It says that a Spanish soldier is a citizen, which meant he had the full rights of someone who had been born into a Roman family.

washed Paul and Silas's wounds, and brought them food and clothes. Then he insisted that he and all his household be baptized at once, and they celebrated for hours.

The next morning Paul and Silas returned to the town's courtroom, where the magistrates smirked to themselves.

"Those strangers will have spent a horrible night in the cells," they said, gloating over their power. "They'll have learned their lesson. Let them go."

Paul and Silas weren't happy at all. They hadn't done anything wrong! They didn't want to creep away.

"We are freeborn Roman citizens," they reminded the jailer. "We want a public apology!"

The magistrates were worried when the jailer told them that they had ordered Roman citizens to be flogged without a trial. They hurried to apologize to Paul and Silas in front of the citizens, before they got in serious trouble. Then the magistrates begged them to leave Philippi. So Paul and Silas went back to Lydia's house in peace, to say goodbye to their friends before continuing on their mission.

Other people might say that Paul and Silas were phoney, but he thought differently. He believed that the two men were truly filled with the power of God.

The jailer gave the order for the other prisoners to be chained up again immediately, but to Paul and Silas's astonishment, he led them out of the prison and back to his own house. In front of his whole household, he fell on his knees before Paul and Silas.

"Tell me what I must do to be saved," the jailer begged.

"Just believe in the Lord Jesus Christ," Paul and Silas replied, "and you will be forgiven for your sins."

The two men told the jailer, his family and servants all about Jesus. When the jailer heard how Jesus wanted His followers to treat everyone with love and kindness, he

Paul arguing
This enamel plaque shows Paul arguing with both Jews and Greeks. Wherever he went, Paul got into debates. He taught that Jesus Christ was the Messiah, the person that God sent to save the people from their sins, and that He had risen from the dead. Many Greeks thought this was a crazy idea, and many Jews found it repugnant. Others believed it and became Christians.

Woman at worship
Many of the first Christians were women. Christianity liberated them, because they were considered by Jesus to be equal to men before God. Women covered their heads when they went into Church. This was an important custom, because at the time only prostitutes had bare heads.

> ❧ **ABOUT THE STORY** ❧
>
> *This is one of many instances in the Bible when something natural – an earthquake in this case – happens at just the right time to help God's servants. It is a miracle of God's timing. God did not stop His servants from being locked up – which was unlawful, without a proper trial – but He did rescue them and at the same time so impressed others with His power that they believed in Him too.*

Paul's Travels and Miracles

PAUL and Silas pressed on to the city of Thessalonika. For three weeks Paul preached in the synagogue to argue that Jesus was the Saviour. Although a large number of people believed, many Jews were outraged. They gathered together a violent mob and went to speak to the city authorities.

"Paul and his companions are trying to turn the world upside down!" they protested. "They're against the Roman emperor, because they say there is another king – Jesus!"

That night, before the Romans took any action, the followers smuggled Paul and Silas out of the city.

> " *And God did extraordinary miracles by the hands of Paul...* "

Paul travelled south to Athens, the main city of Greece. The city was scattered with idols of pagan gods. The streets were full of worshippers taking offerings and sacrifices to and from the pagan temples. Paul strode into the busy market place and preached to passers-by. He also met with philosophers, men who tried to puzzle out the meaning of life and the universe for themselves.

The people of Athens loved nothing more than to hear different beliefs. While many Athenians didn't know what to make of Paul's preaching, others were keen to hear more. They took him to speak on a hill near the vast Acropolis. By the time Paul left Athens, some people had become Christians.

Corinthian capital
A capital is the top of a column that supports a building. The Greeks and Romans loved to build tall columns. They often had rows of them called colonnades. This capital is decorated with a face mask used in the theatre and stylized acanthus leaves under the arms. This design is called corinthian because it came from Corinth.

Helmet
This is a Greek helmet which has lots of protection for the neck, and a central strip to protect the soldier's nose.

Mirror
In biblical times mirrors like this were not made of glass, but of bronze which could be polished so that it gave a good but not perfect reflection. Paul in his letter to the Corinthians says that we see God's truth only dimly, or partially, as in a mirror. When we go to heaven, we shall see God 'face to face'.

Paul's next port of call was Corinth. He stayed with a Jewish couple called Aquila and Priscilla who had fled Rome when the Emperor Claudius had ordered all Jews to leave. Paul preached in the synagogue, and Crispus, the ruler of the synagogue, asked to be baptized. Even so, most of the Jews refused to listen to Paul.

"Your blood be upon your own heads!" Paul cried in the end. "I have done my best with you, and now I will take the message of Jesus Christ to the Gentiles instead."

Paul found that the Gentiles were much more ready to believe in Jesus Christ. Many began asking to be baptized. Then one night, the Lord appeared to Paul in a vision.

"Don't be afraid to speak out in this city, for I am with you," God said. "I will make sure that no harm comes to you, for there are many people here who will turn to me."

Inspired with new faith and courage, Paul stayed for a year and six months in Corinth, and established a strong Christian community there before travelling on to Ephesus, where he stayed for two years.

Everyone who witnessed Paul's miraculous deeds were amazed. In Ephesus, seven sons of a Jewish high priest were so envious that they decided to try it for themselves. They summoned a man who they knew was possessed by an evil spirit, and they tried to cast it out, as they had seen Paul do.

The unearthly voice of the evil spirit wailed, "I know Jesus and I know Paul, but who are you?"

With a howl, the man leapt onto the seven men and they ran from the house.

After that many people who had practised pagan rituals and black magic believed in Jesus.

The third missionary journey of Paul
Paul's third journey was very similar to his second. Once again he revisited the churches of Asia Minor. Paul was a carer as well as an evangelist. He wanted to make sure the Christians were going on with their faith.

❧ ABOUT THE STORY ❧

This story shows how adaptable and flexible Paul was. He did not just take one approach and organize every visit in the same way. He started in the Jewish synagogue if there was one. When he was thrown out of one building he went and hired another. This also shows that his teaching and miracles went side by side. He always began by teaching, but the miracles often helped people believe that Jesus was for real.

Demetrius and the Riot

IN Ephesus, a silversmith called Demetrius made shrines used in the worship of the Greek goddess Artemis. He was unhappy that Paul was turning people away from Artemis, to a religion where they wouldn't need the idols he made. Demetrius called together all the other workmen.

"The numbers of people who worship Artemis are diminishing," Demetrius warned his fellow tradesmen. "It's all due to that Paul. We may lose our livelihoods, and the worship of our great goddess might die out altogether!"

The workmen were outraged at the thought. They set off through the town, shouting, "Artemis of the Ephesians is great!" Soon, people were rushing to the amphitheatre for an emergency public meeting. There was utter confusion. Some people were screaming, "Artemis!", others were yelling, "Praise be to God and His Son, Jesus Christ!", while most people had no idea why they were there.

Paul's followers wouldn't let him enter the amphitheatre for his own safety, and it was several hours before the town clerk managed to quieten everyone down.

"Everyone knows that Ephesus is Artemis's special city!" he yelled. "So why are you getting so worked up over the strangers who have come here? They have said nothing against our goddess. If Demetrius and the craftsmen have a complaint, let them go through the proper legal system. We would be fools to start a riot that would bring the wrath of the Romans down upon us all. Now go home!"

The situation was too fragile for Paul to remain, so he left for Macedonia.

" *Great is Artemis of the Ephesians!* "

◆ ABOUT THE STORY ◆

Many of the clashes between Paul and others started because the Jewish leaders regarded him as a heretic who was stirring up trouble. This story shows that there was a head-on clash between the Christian faith and other religions too. Jesus Himself had said that He was the only way to God. The disciples taught that other religions could not bring people to know God fully and that only Jesus, God's Son, could forgive sins.

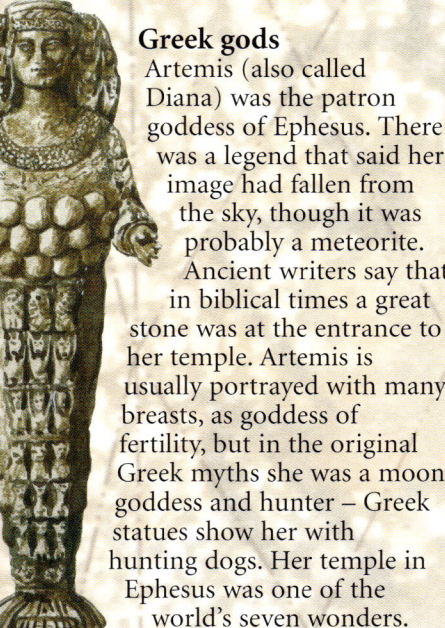

Greek gods
Artemis (also called Diana) was the patron goddess of Ephesus. There was a legend that said her image had fallen from the sky, though it was probably a meteorite. Ancient writers say that in biblical times a great stone was at the entrance to her temple. Artemis is usually portrayed with many breasts, as goddess of fertility, but in the original Greek myths she was a moon goddess and hunter – Greek statues show her with hunting dogs. Her temple in Ephesus was one of the world's seven wonders.

Ephesus
In Paul's day Ephesus was a magnificent city. It housed at least 250,000 people and had an arena that could hold 25,000. A long road flanked with pillars led to the harbour. Paul spent two years here.

Paul in Troas

PAUL decided to return to Jerusalem. He stayed in the city of Troas for a week, encouraging the followers to remain strong and faithful when he had gone. On the night before Paul was due to leave, he spoke well into the evening. No one stirred; everyone hung on his every word. They didn't know how long it would be before the great disciple passed that way again.

On and on spoke Paul. A young man named Eutychus found himself desperately trying to stay awake and listen. Eutychus tried propping himself up in a sitting position in the deep windowsill, opening the window to let in the chill night air, sitting on his hands to make himself uncomfortable, but it was no good. His eyelids began to droop. His head nodded. Finally, he fell fast asleep, lulled by Paul's voice.

> " *He sank into a deep sleep as Paul talked still longer.* "

Everyone was concentrating far too hard on what Paul was saying to notice Eutychus drifting off. In fact, the first they knew of it was when Eutychus fell out of the window and landed with a sickening thud on the ground below. There were horrified gasps as everyone dashed to the window and peered out. Eutychus was lying in a lifeless heap on the floor below.

Paul was the first to race down the stairs and reach the young man. He took Eutychus in his arms.

"Don't worry, his life has now returned to him," Paul reassured everyone.

Amazingly, through the saving grace of the great disciple, Eutychus recovered almost at once. Rejoicing, all the friends made their way back into the house, where Paul continued preaching until daybreak. They didn't stop giving thanks to God even when Paul's ship had sailed into the distance and out of sight.

THE PEOPLE OF TROAS HAD A HUNGER TO LEARN ABOUT GOD. TODAY, SOME PEOPLE TAKE FAITH LESS SERIOUSLY, IT IS A HOBBY RATHER THAN A WAY OF LIFE. CHRISTIANS IN TROAS WOULD BE DISMAYED.

Paul

Like other disciples, Paul was canonized, made a saint, so is depicted with a halo as in this mural from the 1100s from Cyprus. He was a man of great vision and energy. He cared deeply for people but could be a stern critic of those who did not live up to his own strict standards.

❖ ABOUT THE STORY ❖

Paul had a lot of friends with him by the time he reached Troas. Among them were Timothy, who was later to lead the church in Ephesus, and Tychicus, who was like a messenger who went round the churches carrying news from place to place. Luke and several others were with him too. Paul valued the help and support of his friends, although they are not mentioned often in Acts. He did not work alone.

Paul in Jerusalem

PAUL was in a hurry to reach Jerusalem in time for the feast of Pentecost. Yet there were several sad farewells for him to make on the way.

"You won't see me again," Paul told the followers of the Ephesian church. "The Holy Spirit has warned me that suffering and imprisonment awaits me there. I'm not sad. The only reason I consider my life precious is because I can do the work the Lord Jesus Christ has asked me to do. Look after the church when I am gone, for many people will try to destroy your faith and lead you astray. Be alert, and God will give you His help."

At Caesarea, a prophet called Agabus took Paul's girdle and tied up his own hands and feet with it.

"The Holy Spirit has told me that the Jews of Jerusalem will bind you just like this and deliver you into the hands of the Gentiles," warned the prophet, sternly.

Paul's friends protested desperately against Paul continuing on his way. Yet the disciple stood firm.

> " *What are you doing, weeping and breaking my heart?* "

"Don't weep," he begged them. "For I'm ready not only to go to prison for the Lord Jesus Christ – I'm ready to die for Him too."

The moment Paul arrived in Jerusalem, Jesus's brother, James, warned him of trouble. "There are rumours about you," James explained. "We know they're untrue, but others don't. People say that you're encouraging Jews who have converted to Christianity to give up the law of Moses and live like Gentiles!"

Paul did his best to show that the stories weren't true. He began a special week-long Jewish purification ritual, going to the temple every day to pray. Just before the seven days were completed, Paul ran headlong into a group of Jews in the temple who came from a town the disciple had visited on his travels.

"Help, everyone! Help!" they cried.

"This is Paul – the man who is leading Jews everywhere astray!"

To make things worse, earlier on in the day, the same group of Jews had glimpsed Paul in the streets with his Ephesian friend, Trophimus, and wrongly assumed Paul had brought the non-Jew inside the temple.

"Paul has defiled our holy building by smuggling in a Gentile!" the Jews yelled at the tops of their voices.

"Get him!" the men and women shouted, chasing Paul through the temple courtyards and out into the road. The furious people fell on him, punching and kicking him to the ground. Just in time, a Roman tribune burst onto the scene with his soldiers.

"Who is this man?" the tribune asked the crowd, as his soldiers put Paul in chains.

"He has defiled the temple!" some people yelled.

"He has done nothing! Let him go!" screamed others.

"He has broken the law of Moses!" voices roared.

"Rubbish! He's a faithful Jew!" argued still others.

The tribune ordered Paul to be taken back to his barracks. The mob followed, shouting, "Kill him!" When Paul tried to speak to them to explain, they refused to listen to him.

Paul was flung into the cells for the night, and the following morning he found himself hauled out for questioning in front of the Sanhedrin. The disciple held the burning eyes of the Jewish officials in his steady gaze.

"Brothers, I have always lived before God with a good conscience..." he began.

All at once, Paul realized something. The council was made up of half Pharisees, half Sadducees, a Jewish sect who didn't believe in life after death. Paul suddenly saw a way to split the council's opinion and win the Pharisees over to his side.

"Of course," he said, "I myself am a Pharisee. This trial is really about the resurrection of the dead."

The annoyed Sadducees leapt up and began to argue with the Pharisees. Of course, as they were under attack, the Pharisees began to stick up for Paul.

"This man is innocent," some of them began to shout. "We can't find that he's done anything wrong."

At that, the infuriated Sadducees flung themselves on the defiant Pharisees, and the despairing Roman tribune left them to it. He ordered Paul to be taken away again, before the arguing Jews ripped him apart.

Later on, back in the dungeons, Paul heard a voice. It was the Lord calling him.

"Take courage," said God. "For just as you have testified for me here at Jerusalem, so you must also bear witness for me in Rome."

Paul's rescue
This engraving shows the chaos of the Jerusalem riot. Paul was lucky to escape alive.

Caesarea
This city was one of Herod the Great's finest achievements. He built it in honour of the Roman emperor.

❧ ABOUT THE STORY ❧

Paul was getting quite old by now. It would have been quite natural for him to have listened to Agabus and his friends. What was the point of walking into a trap? Paul knew that the path of obedience lay along the way of suffering. In order to achieve all he could for Jesus, and to reach Rome, he had to accept more danger. He had Jesus as his model, who went willingly to the cross. Paul was practising what he preached.

Paul Stands Trial

PAUL was in grave danger. More than forty Jews had sworn not to eat or drink until they had killed the disciple. They hurried off with their plan to the Sanhedrin.

"Ask the tribune to bring Paul down to you again, as if you want to question him further," they suggested. "We'll ambush the soldiers and kill Paul. He'll be off our hands and it won't be your responsibility, either."

The Sanhedrin were pleased with the idea, but Paul's nephew heard the plan and hurried to the barracks to tell the Roman tribune. The tribune was grateful and decided to send the disciple to safety. He wrote a letter to the provincial governor, Felix, explaining that the Jews were after Paul's blood but that he himself couldn't find the disciple guilty of anything deserving death or even imprisonment. That night, Paul was escorted out of the barracks and away by a large number of soldiers.

The Sanhedrin didn't give up. The high priest, Ananias, soon arrived with a spokesman, Tertullus, to put their case before the Roman governor. Tertullus began by trying to persuade Felix with flattery.

"It's thanks to you that we enjoy peace in our province," he said. "This man threatens our stability. He is a ringleader of the sect of Jesus of Nazareth. Now he has broken our law and desecrated our temple!"

Felix brought Paul back to give his side of the story.

"I was only in Jerusalem for twelve days," the disciple began calmly, "and these people didn't find me arguing with anyone or stirring up a riot anywhere in the city. They can't prove any of their accusations except that yes, I worship God according to the way of Jesus Christ. I still believe everything laid down by Jewish law and I was actually purifying myself in the temple, not desecrating it!"

 I appeal to Caesar.

Now Felix was interested in Christianity and he treated Paul kindly. He put off the Jews' demand for a judgement, saying that he wouldn't decide without further investigation, and he put Paul under house arrest, so that the disciple's friends could come and see him. Felix held Paul in this way for two years, during which time he often called the disciple to come and preach to him and his wife, Drusilla, who was a Jew. Finally, Felix was replaced by another governor, Festus, and representatives from the Sanhedrin arrived once again.

❧ ABOUT THE STORY ❧

The Roman governors were unsure what to do about Paul. They were fair, however, and gave him good protection. Paul used his citizen's right to a trial before the emperor more as a way of getting to Rome than anything else. Paul benefited from the Roman system. God's plan had ensured the free and swift spread of Christianity across a wide area in the short space of thirty years.

Synagogue
Paul often began his ministry in synagogues, where people would know of the promised Messiah. Synagogues are Jewish centres for worship, like this one, which is the Great Jerusalem synagogue. They have separate galleries or seating areas for women. The service consisted of prayers, readings and sermons.

Roman census
The Romans organized their empire very efficiently. A group of people called Censors counted all the men who owned property. This shows them at work.

"I have done nothing against the temple, the law of the Jews or against the emperor," Paul insisted. "I ask you not to hand me back to be tried among my enemies. Instead, I claim my right as a Roman citizen to be tried before the emperor himself!"

"Then to Caesar you shall go," replied Festus.

Before he could send Paul off, King Agrippa and his wife Bernice arrived. Festus organized a royal audience, so Agrippa could question Paul too.

Paul was grateful for the chance to explain. He told how he had been a strict Pharisee who had persecuted Christians; how Jesus Christ had spoken to him on the road to Damascus and totally changed his life; and how he had preached to both Gentiles as well as Jews, which was the real reason why so many Jews were seeking his death. Finally, Paul reminded the king of the prophets who foretold that Christ would suffer and rise from the dead, and that He would bring salvation to all the world.

"Paul, all your research into the Scriptures has turned

you mad!" scoffed Festus in a loud voice.

"I am not mad," replied Paul, calmly. "The king knows about these things and I'm sure that he believes in the words of the prophets. Don't you, King Agrippa?"

"Hmm," said Agrippa, thoughtfully. "I think that you're trying to turn me into a Christian in a very short time!"

"Whether now or later, I wish that everyone would become what I am," Paul said with a sad smile, "except for these chains, of course."

Later on, in private, Festus, Agrippa and Bernice went over everything again and again. They all agreed that Paul had done nothing wrong. They sighed. If the disciple hadn't appealed to be tried in Rome, he could have been freed straight away.

Christians fighting the lions
There is a story in the Old Testament of Daniel surviving a night in a lion's cage. Sadly, many Christians in the first two centuries AD did not survive their ordeals with lions. They were thrown to the hungry beasts as 'entertainment' for the crowds.

The Colosseum
This superb theatre in Rome still stands. In Paul's time it held 50,000 people. It was used for gladiator displays.

The Voyage to Rome

PAUL and several other prisoners sailed for Rome, under the protection of a centurion called Julius. Julius treated Paul with great kindness, and when the ship called at Sidon, he let the disciple visit his old friends. Then it was back to the boat for several days' hard sailing to Cyprus, for the wind was against them. Paul wasn't surprised that it was slow-going. He was an experienced sailor and knew that the stormy season was near. On the way to Crete, the ship was beginning to struggle against the gusts and the waves, and they only just made it to a harbour. Paul advised Julius that they should winter there, but the captain and shipowner just scoffed. They assured the centurion that it would be better to winter in a harbour on the other side of the island. As soon as a gentle south wind blew up, they set sail once again, cautiously keeping close to the shore.

The warm breeze didn't last long. A wild north-easterly gale came from behind the mountains, sweeping down over the sea and whipping up the waters, so that the ship was tossed and turned and driven far offshore. As the howling storm went on into the night, the terrified crew slid about the slippery decks trying to lash together the heaving, straining boards of the ship with ropes. Next day, as the waves crashed over the boat, they threw furniture and cargo overboard in an effort to keep afloat. On the third day, as the waves grew yet higher, the desperate crew hurled even spare sails and rigging into the deeps to lighten the load. Day after day, the storm continued to rage round them, showing no sign of ever blowing over. The sailors couldn't remember when they had last glimpsed the sun or the stars. They couldn't tell where the blackness of the sky ended and the blackness of the water began. It felt like the end of the world.

Everyone huddled together in deep despair, certain that they would meet a watery death.

"Take heart," Paul reassured them. "Last night, an angel of God told me that we will eventually run aground and that the ship will go down, but none of us will die."

Finally, during the fourteenth night of the storm, the crew realized the ship was running into shallower water. There was a sudden scramble as they raced to let down anchors, before the boat was tossed onto the rocks that surely lurked in the darkness. At last, there was a glimmer of hope! Everyone wept with relief when the rays of dawn began to light up

the horizon. They had been sure they would never feel the warmth of the sun again. To their joy, they could see land only a little way off. They cast off the anchors and hoisted the foresail and began to make for a bay. As they tried to run ashore, the bow stuck fast in a sandbank. To everyone's horror, the stern of the ship began to break up fast in the crashing surf. There was no other choice but to abandon themselves to the mercy of the sea and jumped overboard before the ship went down.

Incredibly, just as Paul had said, all 276 people made it safely to shore. Some swam. Others floated on broken bits of the ship. The soaked, shivering survivors were welcomed to the island of Malta by the local people, who made a bonfire to warm them up.

> *I now bid you take heart; for there will be no loss of life among you, but only of the ship.*

The locals soon realized that there was something unusual about Paul. An angry viper came slithering out of the fire, trying to escape from the heat, and sank its fangs into his hand. The Maltese people knew that a viper bite was fatal, and they fully expected Paul to die swiftly from the poison. They waited anxiously but nothing happened.

"He must be a god!" they whispered to each other.

The Roman governor of Malta, Publius, was just as generous as his people, and he gave the survivors lodgings in his own quarters. When Paul found out that Publius's father was terribly ill, he healed him to repay the governor's kindness. The news soon got out that the strange man who hadn't died from the snakebite had miraculous healing powers. Maltese from all over the island brought their sick to be cured by Paul. After three months it was time to set sail once again. Paul had won the greatest respect from the people of Malta, and they loaded down the ship with all sorts of provisions and gifts.

Finally, they reached Rome. The other prisoners were handed over to the captain of the guard and imprisoned. Paul, though, was given special treatment. He was allowed to live under house arrest. He awaited trial for two years, and during that time many people came to hear him preach about Jesus Christ and the kingdom of God. Paul also regularly wrote letters to all the friends he had made on his travels, urging them to keep the faith. He continued to do this right up to the very last days of his life, when he knew that he was going to be put to death for the sake of his belief in his master and teacher, Jesus Christ.

Paul's journey to Rome
This took place in the winter of AD59–60. It was not Paul's first experience of shipwreck. Before this journey he had told the Corinthians he had been shipwrecked three times, but did not say where.

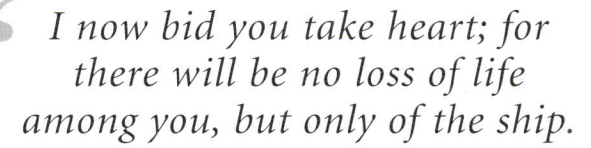

❖ **ABOUT THE STORY** ❖
Sea travel in Paul's day was hazardous. The ships were relatively small, powered only by oars and sails. Navigation was by the stars. Most ships hugged the coast so that they would know where they were. No one sailed in winter, which was where the captain's gamble about the weather failed. Luke, the writer of the story, wants us to see that God would not let His servant die before his work was complete.

The Revelation to John

THE disciple John was in prison on the Greek island of Patmos, praying one sabbath, when he heard a voice filling his mind.

"Write down what I am about to show you and send it to the churches," it instructed.

John spun round to see Jesus Christ behind him, blazing with light brighter than the sun.

"Don't be afraid," Jesus said. "I am the first and the last. I died but I shall live for ever. I hold the keys of death."

John saw a door opening into heaven.

"Come here and I will show you the future of the world," thundered the voice. Suddenly John found himself standing before the very throne of God, surrounded by countless angels singing, "Blessings and honour and glory and might for ever and ever, amen!"

The Lord showed John the mighty battle between good and evil that was being played out on the earth. John saw the happiness of men and women who believe in the salvation of Christ, and the misery and fear of those who do not repent. He saw angels of destruction sweep over the earth to kill wicked men and women with plagues, as warnings to all those left to repent before it was too late. John heard the souls of those who had been killed for their Christian beliefs cry out to God, "O Lord, avenge us and wipe out the world and all its wickedness." God comforted them and told them it was not time.

There were others to come who would win their place in heaven by being martyred in Jesus's name.

John saw a woman representing the people of God giving birth to the Messiah. She stood with the moon under her feet and crowned with twelve stars. Then war broke out in heaven itself. The archangel Michael led God's angels against Satan and his wicked angels, and flung them down from heaven to earth. John watched as the furious Satan and his army went off to tempt all those who follow Jesus's teachings. Great evils rose up, and many people abandoned God to follow Satan. God sent angels over the earth, reminding people that they should fear His judgement and turn again to the Lord while there was still time.

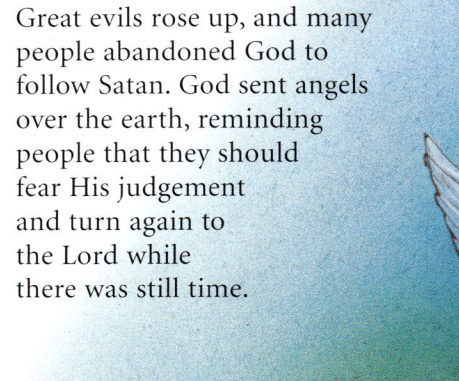

Then John witnessed the end of the world. Jesus, the Lamb of God, was triumphant. There was rejoicing in heaven as Satan was flung into a lake of fire. God then passed judgement on everyone who had ever lived. If their name was not in His book of life, they were destroyed along with Satan.

Finally, John saw a new heaven and a new earth, that looked like the holy city of Jerusalem. The city shone and sparkled as though it was made from diamonds and gold, and decorated with precious jewels in every colour of the rainbow. Through the middle of the city flowed the river of life, as clear as crystal. On either side of the river grew groves of the healing tree of life. The gates of the city stood open, welcoming everything that was good. The city was lit with the glory of God, and there was no temple – because God Himself was there.

"Behold, God is living with all His people in His

> " *I am the Alpha and the Omega, the beginning and the end.* "

kingdom on earth," John heard a voice proclaim. "Pain and sorrow and death are no more."

John heard Jesus Christ speaking to him one last time. "Let all who are thirsty come and drink from the waters of life. I will be coming soon to judge the living and the dead, and the good will be blessed for ever. I am the first and the last, the beginning and the end."

"Amen," whispered John. "Amen!"

A glimpse of heaven
Artists have tried to portray John's vision of heaven with God surrounded by a sea of glass. However, it is really beyond words and imagining.

❧ ABOUT THE STORY ❧

The Book of Revelation is something of a mystery to people today, but in the 1st century AD it was a source of great encouragement. It is largely written in picture language which the Christians of the time would have understood clearly. It is really a series of sketches of the battle between good and evil, which takes place all through human history. It shows that God and His church always triumph in the end.

The Church Since the Apostles

CHRISTIANITY continues to grow around the world. In places, Christianity is growing at an amazing rate. In Russia, and China, for example, Christianity is growing very fast. But the church today is very different. This is how it developed.

Expansion and argument: AD100–700

After the death of the apostles, Paul's prophecy that false teachers would attack the church came true. There were cults such as the gnostics, the forerunners of today's 'new age' movements. These people who did not believe in Jesus were called heretics. They denied important teachings, for example Marcion (d.160) rejected the Jewish elements in the New Testament.

These attacks were countered by writings built on the apostles' teaching. Justin Martyr (c.100–165) defended Christianity against Roman philosophers. The African Tertullian (c.160–225) showed how Jesus could be God and man. In 325 the Council of Nicea defined the basic truths of Christianity (although controversy continued for some time). Despite the arguments and continued persecution, the church grew. In 395 the Roman Emperor Constantine saw a vision of Christ and declared Christianity to be the official religion of the Empire. By 404 the Bible had been translated into Latin, and Augustine of Hippo (354–430) had produced the basis of Christian belief as it is today. Christianity spread across Europe. Columba went to Iona (north-east England) and Saint David converted Wales.

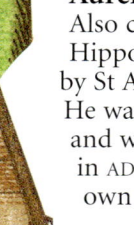

Aurelius Augustinus
Also called Augustine of Hippo, he was baptized by St Ambrose in AD386. He was a great writer, and wrote *Confessions* in AD400, about his own life.

Division and darkness (700–1400)

Then came a period that many Christians today are ashamed of. There were the Crusades, in which western kings tried to force Christianity on countries of the east. There were corrupt popes and clergy who were more interested in worldly wealth than spiritual truth. And in 1054 there was a major split which still exists to this day. The churches of the east (now called the Orthodox Churches) divided from the churches of the west over an important but obscure teaching about the relationship of the Holy Spirit to Jesus Christ.

Crusades
These are the sort of soldiers and knights that fought in the Crusades.

St Thomas Aquinas
He became a monk in 1244, and quickly became a great teacher. His teachings and writings largely represent the teachings of the Catholic Church.

However, there were good points. Thomas Aquinas (1225–74) was an important religious writer whose work is still influential, especially in the Roman Catholic Church. The great cathedrals of Europe were built, including Rheims, Cologne, Salisbury and York. Groups of travelling preachers called for reform and spread the gospel like the first Christians had. Among them was John Wycliffe (1330–84), who was influential in the church going back to believing closely in the detail of the Bible.

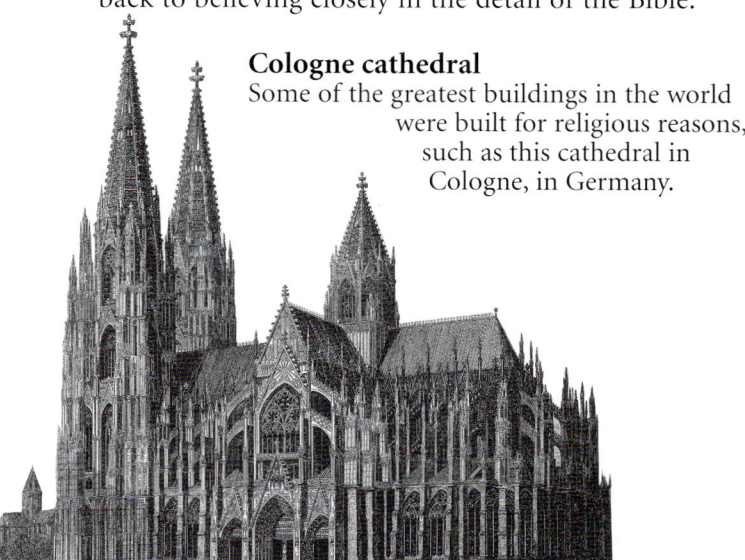

Cologne cathedral
Some of the greatest buildings in the world were built for religious reasons, such as this cathedral in Cologne, in Germany.

Reformation and renewal (1400–1800)

The most famous controversy came when a German monk, Martin Luther (1483–1546) nailed his 95 theses (statements for discussion) on the door of Wittenburg Church in 1517. He criticised many practices and beliefs which, he said, departed from the teaching of the Bible. From then on, other 'Protestants' (protesters) added their voices to his, among them Huldreich Zwingli in Zurich, and John Calvin in Geneva. This period, when the beliefs, or doctrines, of the Curch changed, was called the 'Reformation'.

Martin Luther
Luther's reforms began after a trip to Rome. He disagreed with the sale of indulgences, that is, people buying forgiveness.

The Roman Catholic Church continued under the Pope, but other churches began: Lutherans on the continent, Presbyterians in Scotland, and Anglicans (Church of England) in England. The Reformation in England was a mixture of political and spiritual forces. Henry VIII was glad of an excuse to rid himself of the authority of the Pope so that he could get divorced.

Roman Catholicism continued much the same but Protestantism divided further as groups rediscovered old truths which they emphasised. These divisions were signs of life and vitality. The Baptist churches stressed the need for personal commitment in the rite of baptism. John Wesley (1703–91) founded Methodism when the Church of England disagreed with his open-air preaching and emphasis on spreading the word of Christ.

John Calvin
In 1559 Calvin founded a religious academy in the city of Geneva, Switzerland, which later became a university.

Henry VIII
When the Pope refused to declare that Henry's marriage to his first wife, Catherine of Aragon, was illegal, Henry made himself head of the church, and allowed his own second marriage.

Change and decay (1800–2000)

Over the last 200 years there have been enormous social and cultural changes. 'Enlightenment' thinking (which emphasised the importance of human reason) and the growth of science challenged many Christian beliefs. Only late in the 1900s did western society begin to recognise a 'spiritual' dimension to life.

The Roman Catholic Church made major changes at the Second Vatican Council (1962–5), including allowing mass to be celebrated in local languages and not Latin. The Protestant churches began to talk and work together (and in some cases re-unite), and the World Council of Churches was formed in 1948.

The charismatic (or Pentecostal) movement and the work of evangelists such as Billy Graham have brought thousands of (often young) people into the churches. But it is overseas where the stories of growth which parallel those of the Acts of the Apostles are to be heard today. The missionary movement of the 1800s saw people from the west spread the gospel in Africa, India, China and South America. In the year 2000 there were more Christians (580 million) in Latin America than in Europe (420 million). In Africa, the growth was from 230 million in 1985 to 400 million in 2000. The Holy Spirit is still at work.

Television evangelist
Billy Graham claims to have converted millions of people to Christianity.

Modern Cathedrals
This modern cathedral in Brazil in South America, shows that the Church has a modern and developing outlook. It is an energetic and exciting force in many parts of the world.

Faith, Love and Charity

THE Acts of the Apostles tells of people who risked everything for Jesus Christ. Their example has inspired thousands of Christians in every century since. Others have preached the message of Jesus in new places believing that it is the most important message anyone could ever hear. And still others, inspired by the love of Jesus, have sacrificed all to care for the sick and poor. Some, like the apostles, have even been killed by jealous opponents. Here are a few of their stories.

St Francis of Assisi (*c*.1181 – 1226)

The son of a wealthy Italian cloth merchant, Francis lived a worldly life until he had a vision of Jesus. Then, he gave up everything to teach the gospel. Others joined him in his mission and the Franciscan order of monks was born. He wrote a simple rule of life for their communities, which still exists today. He had a simple faith and a great love of nature.

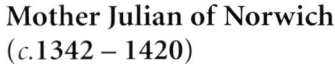

Mother Julian of Norwich (*c*.1342 – 1420)

We do not know anything about Mother Julian's background. She became a hermit devoted to prayer at St Julian's Church in Norwich, in eastern England. She received fifteen visions from God, which she wrote in a famous book *Revelations of Divine Love*. She showed how sinful people could become united with a caring God in a mystical experience of spiritual love.

Elizabeth Fry (1780–1845)

The daughter of a banker in Norwich, she married a merchant. They were Quakers (the Christian group also known as The Society of Friends). She came from a wealthy background, and she was upset by the conditions of women in prison. She began to teach them the Bible, provide them with clothes, and help them to improve themselves. She also campaigned for many prison reforms.

William Booth (1829–1912)

A Methodist from Nottingham, he moved to London but left the church because people did not like his fiery open-air preaching. He was even sent to prison for it. His own mission in the east end of London helped the poor and preached the gospel. In 1878 he formed the Salvation Army, which fought social evils like child labour. The Salvation Army is famous for its social work across the world.

TIMELINE

• Jesus is crucified in Jerusalem by the Roman authorities.

• Matthias is chosen to replace Judas Iscariot as the twelfth apostle.

AD33

DISCIPLES VISITED BY THE HOLY SPIRIT AT PENTECOST

EARLY CHRISTIAN BAPTISM STONE

PENTECOSTAL ALTAR

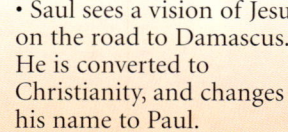

• Peter heals the beggar by the Beautiful Gate.

• Philip baptizes the Ethiopian minister.

• Saul sees a vision of Jesus on the road to Damascus. He is converted to Christianity, and changes his name to Paul.

PETER HEALS AENEAS

Gladys Aylward (1902–1970)

This famous Christian missionary spent all her money on a one-way ticket to China in 1930. In 1938 she helped many children to safety from the China-Japan war. She later ran an orphanage in Taiwan.

Helda Camara (born 1909)

A Roman Catholic priest in Brazil, he became a bishop in 1952 and an archbishop in 1964. He spoken against the bad conditions of the poor, criticising the government and rich landowners whose policies caused the poverty and oppression. He was opposed by some even in his own church.

Mother Teresa of Calcutta (1910 – 1998)

Born in Macedonia in eastern Europe, she was a Roman Catholic nun who worked among the poor children of India. She founded the Sisters of Charity and became a world-renowned figure, always seen dressed in her blue robe. A woman of deep but simple faith, she impressed even the sceptics who came to see her, and was awarded the Nobel Peace Prize in 1979. This is a nun of the Sisters of Charity helping deprived children

Trevor Huddleston (1913–1998)

He went to South Africa, where he worked in Soweto. He became Bishop of Stepney in east London, before being made Archbishop of the Anglican Province of the Indian Ocean. He campaigned actively against apartheid, a system in South Africa of keeping different races apart.

Martin Luther King Junior (1929–1968)

He followed in his father's footsteps to become a Baptist pastor in Montgomery, Alabama, USA. He soon became involved in the struggle for civil rights among his fellow black people. He resigned from his church in 1959 to give all his time to black rights. He spoke for non-violent action and reconciliation between black and white people. This means that he wanted black and white people to get along peacefully. He was murdered by a white man in Memphis, Tennessee in the USA. in 1968. The third Monday in January is celebrated in the USA as Martin Luther King day.

Desmond Tutu (born 1931)

Tutu was made Anglican Archbishop of Cape Town in 1986. He was a passionate campaigner against apartheid, and successfully called on the west to impose economic sanctions (refusing to buy goods) on South Africa. He took a non-violent approach to his protest, and after apartheid fell became Chair of the Truth and Reconciliation Commission, set up to try and overcome the hate and distrust that resulted from apartheid.

PAUL AND BARNABAS WORSHIPPED IN LYSTRA

• The disciples hold a council, and decide to allow Gentiles into the Christian Church.

JERUSALEM

• Paul leaves on his second missionary journey.

• Paul arrested in Philippi

• Riots in Ephesus.

• Paul leaves the city of Troas to return to Jerusalem.

PAUL WRITING HIS LETTERS

EGYPTIAN STATUE OF A PRISONER

• Paul is tried in Jerusalem, and is sent as a prisoner to Rome.

• Paul is martyred in Rome for his belief in Jesus Christ.

AD60

Glossary

apostle

The group of twelve men that Jesus picked from His disciples were called apostles. They were the closest people to Him, and learned the most from Him. The group of apostles also includes Saul, who converted to Christianity after Jesus's death, and became Paul.

baptism

Jesus commanded that His followers be baptized to show they had been converted. Baptism involves immersing people in water. John the Baptist baptized many people as a sign of repentance and inner cleansing. The apostle Paul later said that Christian baptism is symbolic. When the person disappears beneath the water and then reappears, they are symbolically undergoing death, burial and resurrection, as Christ did.

disciples

As Jesus travelled round Galilee, teaching and preaching to the people there, people started to follow Him and His way of living. These people were called disciples. From the larger group of the disciples, Jesus chose his particularly close group of followers, called the apostles.

Gentile

This is a general term for nations, and which came to mean anyone who is not Jewish. Jesus made sure that he preached His message to Gentiles as well as Jews.

Gospel

Some of the people who followed Jesus's teaching recorded His life and works in writing. These are known as the Gospels, which means "good news". These writings have been passed down through the years and now form part of the New Testament. The Gospels are credited to Matthew, Mark, Luke and John.

kingdom of God

The kingdom of God is not an earthly kingdom. Jesus said that the kingdom of God is within everyone who follows His teachings, and tries to live their life in a Christian way.

Messiah

This means anointed one in Hebrew. The word Christ is the equivalent word in Greek. It means one chosen by God. By the time of Jesus, all the Jews were hoping for a great Messiah-king to set up an everlasting kingdom. Jesus's kingdom, the kingdom of God, was not an earthly kingdom. Jesus was not an emperor commanding armies as many were expecting. The kingdom of God will last forever.

ministry

Jesus spent about three years travelling around Judea, teaching the people about how they should live their lives and respect God. This is called His ministry.

miracle

Jesus performed many miracles during his ministry in Galilee healing the sick and dying, casting out demons, and even bringing people back from the dead. Miracles are sometimes described as "mighty works", and they are performed through the power of God.

parable

Jesus told stories to people, called parables, to teach them about the kingdom of God. The stories used people and situations that his audience would be familiar with, which made the point of Jesus's story easier for people to remember and to understand.

Pharisee

A strict religious sect, the name Pharisee means "separated ones". They were generally ordinary people, not priests, who closely followed Jewish law. Sometimes they extended the ways that these laws were applied to make them even harder to follow. For example, when they said that people must not work on the Sabbath, they meant people could not walk more than about 1km from their house, they could not carry a heavy load or even light a fire in their house.

repentance

If a person repents, it means that they are truly sorry for their sins. Jesus forgave the sins of those people who came to Him and were genuinely sorry for what they had done. But it also means being determined to leave sin behind, trying not to sin at all in future.

resurrection

Three days after Jesus died on the cross, He came back to life, He was resurrected. This is the main and central point of the New Testament, and of Christianity.

Sadducees

This was a smaller group of people than the Pharisees, but more influential. Most of them were members of the family of priests. Most of the information that we have comes from their enemies so is not very reliable. We do know that they did not agree with the extensions of the law that the Pharisees tried to impose on people. This is why the Sadducees did not believe in life after death, as this is not mentioned in the Old Testament.

Samaritan

When the Promised Land was conquered by the Babylonians the Jews were taken away to live in Babylon, a period known as the Exile. The city of Samaria was filled with people from other lands, taken there by the Babylonians. These people were hated by the Jews after this time for taking the Jews' cities. Jesus makes sure that He demonstrates his concern for them, and shows that the kingdom of God is open to everyone by using the Samaritans in his stories.

synagogue

In Jesus's time Jews went to the synagogue to worship, just as they still do today. The synagogue had separate seating for men and women. It also served as the school for Jewish children.

Index